SYSTEMS OF PUBLIC WELFARE

SYSTEMS OF PUBLIC WELFARE

BY

HOWARD W. ODUM
KENAN PROFESSOR OF SOCIOLOGY AND
DIRECTOR OF THE SCHOOL OF PUBLIC WELFARE
UNIVERSITY OF NORTH CAROLINA

AND

D. W. WILLARD
ASSOCIATE IN RESEARCH
LINCOLN SCHOOL OF TEACHERS COLLEGE
COLUMBIA UNIVERSITY

CHAPEL HILL
UNIVERSITY OF NORTH CAROLINA PRESS
1925

PRESSES OF
THE SEEMAN PRINTERY INCORPORATED
DURHAM, N. C.
THIS BOOK WAS DIGITALLY PRINTED.

CONTENTS

LIST OF CHARTS

PREFACE

ONE of the most difficult problems of public administration in the United States is that centering around departments, bureaus, and boards of public welfare. Perhaps there is no field in which accurate information and dependable direction are more eagerly sought by old and new officials alike. Likewise, legislative bodies, civic and social agencies, and citizens in general are earnestly seeking for information and examples which will point to best administrative methods. This is true not only because of the difficulties involved in the problems of public welfare and relief, but also because of the very large amount of public moneys expended and because successful administration of public welfare lies at the very heart of the American ideal to make democracy effective in the unequal places.

This volume is presented, therefore, as a small effort to meet such a demand for comprehensive information concerning the scope, organization, and administration of state systems of public welfare in the United States. Parts of chapters 1, 6, and 7 appeared in the January 1924 *Annals* of the American Academy of Political and Social Science, pages 1, 93 and 137. Parts of chapters 2, 8, and 11 have appeared in the *Journal of Social Forces*. We wish to thank Miss Breckinridge,

Mr. Jensen, Mr. Kelso, Mr. Conant, Mr. Bates, and Mr. Parsons for their original contributions and for permission to use them in this volume. We wish to thank also Professor J. F. Steiner and Miss Katharine Jocher for valuable suggestions.

The volume is not intended as an exhaustive treatise. Although charts and information have been checked up approximately to 1925 through documents and correspondence; and although the general descriptions of charts are relatively correct, there will be of course minor variations due to omissions and recent changes. This will not, however, affect the real purpose and plan of the volume which is to present the aggregate picture. It is hoped, therefore, that the information contained in the book may be of use to the many states now seeking to organize and perfect their systems, as well as to general students of public welfare and social work. If, besides, it may contribute a little toward clearing up common misunderstandings concerning public welfare it will have added value.

—H. W. O.
—D. W. W.

Chapel Hill, N. C.
June 20, 1925.

CHAPTER I

THE NEW PUBLIC WELFARE

IN the history and development of public welfare two strange anomalies appear. One is the almost universal tendency of human society to neglect the study and promotion of its own welfare and adequacy until it has first studied and promoted all things else. The other is the similar uniform habit and tendency toward carelessness, inefficiency, and even graft in the administration of public relief and corrections. Both are absurd and unreasonably illogical. Nevertheless, these are the facts which we have had to face. Just as the study of society was the last of the sciences to develop, so the scientific study and treatment of social deficiencies seems to be the hardest of all tasks to get under way. And, like the police departments of our large cities, traditional breeding grounds for inefficiency, waste and corruption, so public charities and public welfare seem most prone to catch up the straggling threads of loose thinking, non-progressive inertia and stubborn attitudes towards the normal evolution of democratic ideals.

There is now at last, however, a vigorous turn for the better. What was a decade ago a new ideal in the form of departments of public welfare is now coming to be a matter of fact. The burdened taxpayer is coming to realize something of the importance of having self-support in public institutions and of effecting economies in their administration. The public is also coming to realize that self-respect, earning capacity, rebuilding of character and fortune are the normal and logical expectation of society's unfortunates. The taxpayer as well as the social worker is learning that it is more economical to keep people out of institutions than to put them in and try to reduce cost after they are in. In all of these processes, together with many others, the old ideas of charities and corrections with their manifold opportunities for waste and inefficiency have given way to the better concepts of public welfare in which protection, preservation and development, through preventive methods, take the place of the old remedial and endless processes. In all of these processes there will be found a very definite philosophy and important technique of government.

At the outset the fact should be emphasized that by "public welfare" is meant, not simply "welfare" or "human welfare" or "social welfare"; but that very definite service of democratic government which provides organization, technique and means for making democracy effective in the unequal places—effective in extended application as well as in ideals, written laws and statutes, and in constitutional provisions. Like "public education," "public welfare" constitutes a very distinctive concept and service. What public education was to the last half of the last century in the development of the democratic ideal, public welfare may well be to the first half of this century. Indeed it seems very probable that progress in the field of public welfare will constitute the outstanding contribution of the half century toward progress in American democracy. But like public education, long considered unnecessary, dangerous and bringing the stigma of charity to its recipients, public welfare must needs take its time to get under way, and must be misunderstood, misinterpreted and surrounded by limitations that impede its progress. It so happens, therefore, that there is perhaps no aspect of public service today that needs interpretation more than public welfare.

Public welfare is a definite part of government. No student of modern conditions will doubt the need of classifying with governmental efforts a division of public service upon which approximately one-fifth of the total general state funds and appropriations is being expended. Nor will he doubt the advisability of working out effective organization and technique for bringing about a larger service and a greater economy in the expenditure of these public moneys. If, on the other hand, the organization and administration of public welfare on efficient and scientific bases can actually save the government money and increase its efficiency in connection with its other divisions of service, the appeal for recognition is twofold. It is very clear that the old "charities and corrections" have been transcended by the newer reasonable, democratic, constructive and preventive, as well as remedial, service to all the people within the state's domain. It is equally clear that the obligation to make good in these newer steps of progress rests alike upon formal government and civil community; upon public officials and public service departments; and upon private voluntary agencies and social workers.

The scope and meaning of public welfare may be stated in other illustrative ways. Public welfare may be the last and perfecting stage in an effective democracy. Or again, public welfare may be to the ideals of a modern complex industrial American democracy what the first constitution was to the ideals of the early pioneers—a definite organization and means to give form and effectiveness to the ideals which they sought to make good. Democratic ideals, and even democratic laws and statutes, writ well in the capitols of state and nation, or embodied in the literature of a growing people—apart from life—will scarcely become permanent enactments if they do not reach the unequal places and the unequal folk. In a nation of very large and rapidly growing population of heterogeneous elements; of a very large and complex industrial development; of a very large and complex urban evolution; and of still larger areas of isolation and rural regions standing out, not as formerly alongside similar areas the country over, but in contrast to more developed sections, the inequality of "equality of opportunity" is likely to become the dominant characteristic unless there be developed a definite organization and technique to take care of such evolution and change. The great state papers of Washington and Lincoln and the others of the past have been great because America has "made them good" through enacted government. The ideals and objectives expressed in later periods can become great and effective only in proportion as they are "made good" by an enacted government and citizenship keeping pace with normal social growth and change.

The problem of the unequal places and unequal folk may be illustrated in scores of incidents and conditions in the very natural and normal development of American life today. The fault is not with growing America but with the inability or lack of disposition to have governmental and community services keep pace with inevitable progress. In past generations the assumption has seemed a natural one that inequality of opportunity was inevitable alongside inequalities in nature and nurture such as a normal life and society everywhere manifest. The newer ideals of democratic government were set forth in opposition to such assumptions. And yet these newer ideals will be without form and void, and inequality of opportunity will grow rather than decrease unless there be worked out perfecting steps through which such ideals may be interpreted and enacted for all the people in whatever areas and in whatever conditions. There may be at the National Capitol or at the state capitol most excellent laws on compulsory school attendance, for example; laws designed to give all children an equal opportunity for education and development. But if there be outside and remote areas in which the people are not even aware of such laws; in which they do not and cannot know the meaning of such laws; or in which educational facilities are unequal; or in which social surroundings and inheritance are such as to make impossible the enactment of stated ideals of equality of opportunity, the attempt to enforce such a law but engenders a bitter minority, honestly and pathetically wondering what it is all about. This is true in other matters, such as the treatment of crime and minor criminals; in the matters of poverty and ignorance; in the matters of public health, of industry and of many matters pertaining to the freedom and the pursuit of happiness. It is true not only in isolated rural areas, but in congested city and industrial areas; it is true in the case of foreign elements of the population, and it is true in the case of great complex industries and city populations; and it is true wherever there is not a balance as between agriculture and commerce, capital and labor, big business and community life, town and country, the people and government, extremes and means.

In proportion to the increase of this minority in the unequal places, whether in numbers or in the degree of inequality, it would seem a fair hypothesis to affirm that the ideals and enactments of democratic government were not being made effective. This is true in more ways than one. It is true because the very principles of the democratic ideal, or, if you please, the democratic religion or philosophy, are being violated in both theory and practice. But it is true in an even more definite and forceful way. Whenever this minority of inequality tends to become a majority of discontent and of unknowing representatives of state or nation, existing government will tend to be overthrown and the age-long cycle begins over again. Herein lies the great contribution of community to government. It may well be assumed that no state or national government, no matter how sincere and active in its endeavors to render democratic services, can succeed by the mere enactment of laws and statutes on its legislative pages. Nor can any large and modern state or nation hope from a centralized and formal headquarters alone to interpret and enact its government. This is true, if for no other reason, because of the physical impossibility of reaching all the elements within its domain. It is true further, because it violates the whole principle of civic cooperation and citizen participation in government, which is the essential basis of democracy. What is needed, therefore, is a guarantee that each social unit—state, county, smaller community—shall say in substance and in fact to the larger governmental unit: "We underwrite for this area and this people, through local government and civic cooperation, the task of both interpreting and carrying out the ideals and standards of democratic governmental services." This principle has been assumed, of course, in our own government in its great approximation of the democratic ideal; and we have approached the ideal more nearly than has been the case in other times and by other governments. The problem now is to work out such definite organization and administrative means as will complete the services heretofore represented through public education, public health, public protection, and other forms of governmental coöperation as well as governmental coercion. Public welfare in its attempt to minister to the socially deficient, on the one hand, and to the unequal places to prevent social deficiency on the other, offers a next step. Public welfare, therefore, instead of becoming a form of centralized and paternalistic government, emerges as the opposite contribution of community to government, provided it has, of course, adequate organization, technique and standardized methods of operation. To state the problem negatively, the question may well be raised as to what, if not public welfare, in this sense, will prevent our own efforts in democracy from going the way of past efforts or of fulfilling the predictions of the pessimists as soon as our civilization reaches its more complex and difficult stages.

There is another important way in which public welfare may contribute largely to effective democracy. It has been the custom to consider democracy under two general divisions: The general philosophy of equal opportunity and the technique of government through which the ideals of such a philosophy are to be attained. But too often in the philosophy itself and in the social machinery for its effective achievement the whole concept has been too largely limited to political democracy. To seek political equality and equality of social opportunity for adults whose heritage, family life and opportunities for development have been woefully deficient is to offer a poor substitute for the fullness of life. To offer only a representative part in government through the ballot to those whose lives may be handicapped or broken through unequal struggles in industry is to offer a substitute for democracy. To violate the original American principles of religious freedom through intolerance and persecution or through constant religious conflict and strife, even though political representation may be unimpaired, would be going backward and not forward. To offer as a substitute for democratic government a centralized bureaucratic service or dictation by an intellectual aristocracy, or "super legislation" and censorship, is un-American, and also violates the principle of community participation in government. And thus it is with educational democracy and its several aspects. The important fact is that democracy is as many-sided as is life, and that to attain it, not only a philosophy, but a social organization adequate for life must be developed.

For the purpose of analysis and for the presentation of the papers in this volume public welfare may be said to contribute to a sixfold democracy of equal opportunity corresponding to the six major institutional modes of life: organic democracy, conforming to the home and family; educational democracy, conforming to opportunities offered through the school and education; political democracy, representing the state and government; religious democracy, representing the church and religion; industrial democracy, representing industry and work; and social democracy, representing the ideals of community and association. It seems clear that no one of these alone can be adequate, either for itself or for the development of the component parts. Industrial democracy can no more be taken for the whole, than can work be counted all of life. Religious freedom is worth little if children may not be born well, grow in health, develop in stature; if mothers and wives in isolated or congested areas must toil in an unequal distribution of life and labor as between men and women, as between neighborhood and families. The great American boast that men may rise from simple beginnings to greater leadership amounts to little if communities may poison youth with vice or idleness or injustice in the courts. Freedom to go to school, or compulsory laws to enforce attendance are pitifully weak in comparison with an effective family welfare service which instructs and leads into the knowledge of what education means and into the desire to attain it. Labor proclamations about participation in the government of industry are worth little compared to the coöperative enactment of an industrial welfare which prevents child labor, unsanitary conditions and the other inequalities which may arise because of the lack of understanding and coöperation on the part of all concerned. In all these aspects of human endeavor public welfare may be expected to make great contributions to progress; and it may be affirmed equally that without an effective public welfare service of this sort, there can be no maximum achievement toward the attainment of human development and human freedom.

The most outstanding example of the new philosophy and technique of public welfare will be found in the organization of state departments. City departments are important, but as yet they represent only special cases and special situations. County organizations are important as a part of the organic system underlying state organization and administration. It would seem most important, therefore, that larger efforts be undertaken to see that the state systems of public welfare in the United States be put upon some such substantial basis as are the state departments of education, of which every state has its definite organization and its definite administrative head. To study more fully, therefore, as much as possible of the present situation and of present organizations in the United States becomes an important task to which social workers, students of politics and public policy will more and more devote themselves.

CHAPTER II

HISTORY AND DEVELOPMENT OF STATE SYSTEMS OF PUBLIC WELFARE

A STUDY of the development of state public welfare systems shows a chaotic variety of experiments. There are few points on which there is anything like universal agreement among the states except perhaps on the point that the field of service is one to be recognized as a branch of the state organization, and even on that point three states have not acquiesced and have not yet created a state agency for such service.[1]

The movement toward creation of a central or state agency for standardizing the care, custody, and treatment of persons in distress and recognized as appropriate subjects for public service was begun in Massachusetts in 1863 when the legislature created a Board of State Charities, with powers of supervision and recommendation in relation to the charitable and correctional institutions already established and with administrative powers in the matter of admittance, transfer, and discharge of pauper lunatics.[2] Massachusetts

---

[1] Mississippi, Nevada, and Utah. Utah has had for some time, however, a commission of inquiry on the subject.

[2] Massachusetts Acts of 1863, chap. 240. A more correct view would probably regard the creation in 1847 of the New York State Emigration Commission, followed in 1851 by the Massachusetts Board of Alien Passengers and State Paupers, as the initial step in the field (see E. Abbott, "Restrictive Immigration Legislation," *Proceedings of the National Conference of Social Work*, 49th Annual Meeting, 1922).

was followed by Ohio and New York in 1867; Illinois, North Carolina, Pennsylvania, and Rhode Island in 1869; Wisconsin and Michigan in 1871; and Kansas and Connecticut in 1873.

It is not profitable to list the authorities in the order of their creation.[3]   The United States Census *Summary of Laws relating to Dependent Classes* makes possible a statement with reference to the situation in 1913 sufficiently complete for present purposes. The names of the authority created vary from state to state and from time to time in the same state, and differences in name indicate a wider or a narrower scope of work entrusted to the newly created body as well as the nature of the power given. The Board of Public Welfare created in 1919 in Georgia[4] exercises powers that are "strictly visitorial and advisory." The Illinois[5] department is one of nine executive departments of the state. The Board of State Charities of Massachusetts,[6] for example, created, in 1863, to deal with the state institutions and with the state "poor" who had no "settlement," became in 1879 the State Board of Health, Lunacy and Charity, when the correctional functions were assigned to the Board of Commissioners of Prisons (Laws of 1879, chap. 249), five in number, of

---

[3] Nor is it implied that all these authorities have had continuous effective existence. In some states there have been intervals when the law was repealed; in others, failure to appropriate has for the time rendered the legislation nugatory.

[4] Georgia Acts of 1919, No. 186, sec. 6.

[5] Illinois Revised Statutes, chap. 24½, sec. 3.

[6] Massachusetts Acts of 1879, chap. 291.

whom two were women, was revived in 1886 as
the State Board of Lunacy and Charity,[7] relieved
of certain tasks connected with lunatics and settled
paupers in 1898,[8] when it became the State Board
of Charity, which it remained until erected, in
1919, into a Department of Public Welfare.[9] As
to structure, it may be noted that in 1913, when all
the states except ten[10] had created these authorities, thirty-five of the thirty-eight established[11]
were in the forms of boards varying in number
from three to twelve. Of these thirty-five boards,
twenty-one were state boards of charities or of
charities and corrections,[12] seven were boards of
control,[13] while in five states[14] there had been
adopted the plan of two boards, one salaried and
executive known as the Board of Administration,
the other unsalaried and supervisory known as a
Charities Commission.

[7] Acts of 1886, chap. 101.

[8] Acts of 1898, chap. 433.

[9] Acts of 1919, chap. 350. Among the fifteen departments created there
were Departments of Mental Diseases, Corrections, Public Health and
Education.

[10] Alabama, Delaware, Georgia, Idaho, Mississippi, Nevada, New Mexico,
South Carolina, Texas and Utah. Delaware had a Tuberculosis and a Blind
Commission, and Texas had a State Bureau of Child and Animal Protection.

[11] Oklahoma provided in its constitution for a commissioner of state charities; New Jersey had a commission of charities and correction; Alabama
had an inspector of jails, almshouses and cotton mills; Kentucky had an
inspector of institutions in addition to a state board and is not counted.

[12] Arkansas, Colorado, Connecticut, Florida (board of commissioners state
institutions); Indiana, Louisiana, Maine, Maryland (state aid and charities);
Massachusetts, Michigan, Missouri, Montana (charities and reform); New
Hampshire, New York, North Carolina, Pennsylvania, Rhode Island, South
Dakota, Tennessee, Virginia, Wyoming, See Census Summary State Laws
relating to Dependent Classes, p. 316 fol.

[13] Arizona, Iowa, Kansas, Kentucky, New Hampshire, Washington and
West Virginia.

[14] California, Illinois, Minnesota, Nebraska, Ohio.

These authorities were created to meet two
great groups of problems: (1) the diversity of
practice, inadequacy of equipment, competitive relationships and often wasteful methods characteristic of the care of wards for whom institutions,
whether state or local, had been established;[15] and
(2) the same lack of uniformity, the same inadequacy of service, the same wastefulness characteristic of the "outdoor" care of persons in distress
given by the local authorities. The object sought
was declared to be "to secure the economical and
efficient administration" of the public charitable
and correctional institutions and agencies[16] for
the purpose of reducing suffering, preventing
needless misery and lessening the burden of the
taxpayer.

The movement was a natural and inevitable one
based, in general, on sound governmental principles. Its progress was, however, impeded by two
sets of influence. One influence was that of inertia, inexorably resulting from the number of
state legislatures and from the historical and accidental character of the organization in the various
states. The other was an influence growing out
of the nature of the problem involved; those who
were peculiarly moved to improve the service of

---

[15] In Massachusetts, for example, in 1863, beside the local almshouses and
local prisons there were three state almshouses, a state hospital on Rains-
ford Island, three state lunatic asylums, a state prison, a state reform school,
a state industrial school for girls, and a School Ship (Massachusetts), and,
partially controlled by the state, the Massachusetts General Hospital, the
Massachusetts School for the Blind and the Massachusetts School for Idiots.

[16] To quote from the act creating the first Massachusetts board.

the poor, sick, mentally feeble, and delinquent were also often especially concerned to keep that service free from the weaknesses of ordinary governmental standards and recognized the peculiar opportunity for graft and mismanagement in the very nature of the tasks undertaken.

The necessity of obtaining the acquiescence of forty-eight legislatures in a program of regard and treatment for the least influential members of the community has placed a heavy burden on those urging the advance. The fear of giving over the poor to new forms of exploitation has led sometimes either to acquiescence in continued incapacity or to the proposal of complicated arrangements not only for securing governmental action, but also for keeping that action constantly under a critical and supervisory scrutiny.

There arose, therefore, early in the development of the authorities, two schools of thought: first, that school whose confidence might be said to rest on consent, who urged the value of the supervisory agencies, unpaid, divorced from partisan politics, having nothing in the way of patronage to offer, and recognizing that ultimate care for the helpless must lie in sympathy, pity, good will and intelligence; on the other side were ranged those who might be said to be dominated by the ideals of efficiency, who chafed at delay, were shocked at the waste, were confident that organization and administration could hasten the accomplishment of the purposes they all sought.

It was impossible that the authority created should exercise no power. Visitation, inspection, reporting, suggesting are themselves incisive powers and further development was inevitable.[17] And in 1887 at the National Conference of Charities and Correction, Mr. Sanborn, the great executive of the Massachusetts board during the early years of its existence, pointed out that of the twelve state boards then in existence only three or four remain simply advisory in their power and duties, although originally most of them were so established, at least in theory. The Boards of New York, Pennsylvania, Illinois, Michigan, Wisconsin and doubtless of some other states were created with duties of inspection and supervision and with powers of advice and recommendation, and only these; but, in all these states, it has been found necessary or expedient to add executive powers, and to make these Boards, in fact (what those of Massachusetts, Rhode Island, Kansas, and Minnesota have always been in name), a part of the state administration. In New York, for example, executive powers in regard to the support of state paupers and the removal of immigrants and vagrants have been conferred; in Pennsylvania, these powers, and also the summary

---

[17] In fact, as early as 1881, Wisconsin took the step of creating a Board of Supervision of Charitable, Reformatory and Penal Institutions, abolishing the boards of trustees of the state institutions, without disturbing the State Board of Charities and Reform, created in 1873 and abolished only in 1891, when the present Board of Control was established. *See* Laws of Wisconsin, 1881, chap. 298; 1891, chap. 221.

powers of a Lunacy Commission; in Illinois, very extensive powers of audit; in Wisconsin, the power of the purse over the maintenance of the insane poor in county asylums; in Michigan, executive powers in regard to children placed in families. The Rhode Island Board, which was at first made partly executive and partly advisory, has now complete control of all the state establishments. In Massachusetts, the executive powers of the Board which were from the first extensive, have been enlarged until it is now one of the most important branches of the state administration.

These changes in the function of the Boards are not the result of chance, but indicate what we believe to be the fact, that such authority, when once created in a state, will naturally increase; for occasions arise when power must be lodged somewhere, and no more suitable place can be found for it. No changes, so far as we know, have been made in the other direction—of limiting the duties of these Boards—except when special Boards have been created to relieve the Board of Charities of some part of its increasing duties; and we believe there is no State Board now in existence which possesses less power than when it was first established. This indicates that the confidence originally reposed in them has been justified by their activity.[18]

---

[18] *Proceedings*, 14th Annual Meeting (1887), p. 103.

However, the rate at which the development toward control should take place, the significance in the changes proposed and put through, the perils of relying rather on authority than on developed intelligence, sympathy and conscience were subjects that could not be ignored in the presence of the great advocates of the conservative school.   There were giant figures in those days playing great rôles on the stage of public charitable service; and the voices of Roeliff Brinkerhoff, Timothy Nicholson, F. H. Wines, F. B. Sanborn, Mrs. Josephine Shaw Lowell, still ring out across the years, pointing on the one hand to the peril of letting in the wolves, of overemphasizing the need of economy,[19] a term far from clear, when the word "adequacy" had hardly been introduced into the social workers' vocabulary and on the other hand of losing the whole force of local initiative.   At the National Conference of 1902, for example, it was urged:

In states where the central board (commonly called a board of charities) is a supervisory board, and the administration of the state institutions is confided to individual boards of trustees or managers, the system adopted secures the benefits

---

[19] The reports are, of course, from the beginning to the present times filled with pleas for a realization of the differences between true and false economy. *See, e.g.,* the *36th Annual Report of the New York State Board* (1902), pp. 15-16; or the *Second Biennial Report of the Kansas State Board of Administration* (1920), p. 8.   The great discussion, however, and the great comparison between the relative efficiency of actual control as compared with supervision at its best is Mr. Henry C. Wright's classic study of the Methods of Fiscal Control of State Institutions, made for the New York State Charities Aid Association in 1911, now out of print.

both of responsibility in the discharge of executive functions and also of independent inspection, criticism and suggestion. In states where the central board is a board of control, the administration of the state institutions may be equally good, or it may be worse or better; but there is no adequate supervision of their methods and results. In other words, the loss is certain, but the gain is problematical.

*   *   *   *

The proposal to establish a central board of control usually originates, I think, in the brain of some scheming politician, who wishes to strengthen a political machine by the addition to it of the state charitable institutions, which can be effectively used by an adroit and unscrupulous political manager as an aid to the control of caucuses, primaries and conventions, and in the carrying of elections. They can of course be far more effectively used for this purpose if they have a single head, himself a member of the machine and in sympathy with its general aims. The motive which prompts the suggestion is concealed, and the ostensible motive put forth is the intention to secure better business organization, improved business methods, which appeals to business men, not politicians, and who claim still less to be experts in benevolent work. Into the hands of these schemers those reformers play, who are impatient because reforms grow slowly, with the gradual education of public opinion, upon which they at last depend for moral support, and who imagine that they can be effected by the concentration of authority in a board which can issue and enforce the necessary orders. But does not this authority, this power, already exist? Why is it not used? Why suppose that one set of men will accomplish what several sets of men working in harmony cannot accomplish?

A central supervisory board is apt to be far more active and efficient than a board of control in the matter of arousing public interest in the benevolent work, both of the state and of private individuals or associations, and of educating public opinion on social questions as related to public and private charity. It is natural, is it not, that an executive board which believes itself to be doing all that can or ought to be done, with the means and facilities at its disposal, should be indifferent to public opinion or sensitive to criticism of its methods by the community? But a supervisory board, whose function is criticism, welcomes and stimulates the closest inspection of public and private charities by the public at large, feeling that in such inspection it receives moral support of inestimable value to the state.

Personally I dread the creation of centralized boards of control. They are less objectionable if they have charge only of single groups of institutions, as, for instance, all the hospitals and asylums for the insane or all the prisons. They are also less objectionable in small states than in the larger ones. They would be very much less objectionable if they did not mean the abolition of the supervisory boards but two central boards cannot ordinarily be maintained in one state. If they could there would almost inevitably exist rivalry and conflict between them.[20]

Stress was laid, on the other hand, on the possibility of reduced cost, of increased accuracy of accounting, of greater uniformity of reporting, of the elimination of local authorities, of improved service, of better discipline among employees, of relief given executives of institutions from financial problems, of the elimination of party politics, of the equitable assignment of the state's resources among the various institutions and of the general advantage of applying to charitable service principles worked out in the field of business.[21]

These arguments are, of course, unanswerable. The necessity of an authoritative central agency is now fully recognized, and the question is now rather to what extent is public opinion prepared and in what form is the power to be granted. These divergencies of opinion, found determining the phrasing of the most recent legislation, ex-

[20] *Proceedings of the National Conference of Charities and Correction,* 29th Annual Meeting (1902), p. 147.
[21] *See,* especially, *Proceedings of the National Conference of Charities and Corrections,* 31st Annual Meeting (1904), pp. 180, 181.

press themselves in the terms supervision, control, management, administration, terms that now may be said to represent difference in degree rather than in kind of authority. And so, as these controversies have continued or have been renewed the tendency to which Mr. Sanborn referred in 1887 has continued, new laws have been enacted, old ones have been amended with great variations in the degree to which the central authority has been given power and as to the kind of power bestowed but moving, on the whole, toward a greater incisiveness and in general toward a wider range of control.[22]

A further word should be said at this point concerning the devices authorized on the part of the central authority. They are in general, visitation, inspection, prescribing forms for record-keeping, formulating rules and regulations, requiring reports, granting permission for organization, periodic certification, granting licenses, with or without the power of revocation, compulsory conference and consultation, selection of personnel by nomination, appointment or confirmation, requiring estimates of expenditure in advance, approval of accounts, sharing the cost when the work is approved, meeting the entire cost.

The great questions then have been (1) to what extent was the mere force of central knowledge

---

[22] This does not mean that the particular authority known as "public welfare" has been given wider powers, but that wider service in meeting the needs of persons in distress is undertaken by the state.

with its possibility of publicity adequate, and to what extent should be granted such other powers as have been enumerated, especially those related to purchasing and to the selection of personnel; (2) to what extent should the central authority stimulate, encourage and standardize the institutional and local organizations and to what extent should those organizations be absorbed; (3) when should agencies specialized by function be created and relieve the agency attempting to deal with many groups of wards; (4) what should be the relationships among these services, those allocated on the basis of function and those allocated on the basis of ward; (5) how could the supervisory and critical element so emphasized in the early days be retained as the organization took on more and more the orthodox hierarchical governmental form; (6) how, in an economic and industrial system under which the wage scale leaves great numbers of persons below the level of adequate living, can the doctrine of adequate care for the wards of the state be reconciled with the apparent interests of the taxpayer?

In the face of these questions, the present organization of the central authority in the various states may be briefly summarized.[23]

---

[23] As has been said, such a summary is far from adequate. As to its accuracy, one can plead only every effort to secure accuracy by consultation with the session laws since 1913, by personal inquiry since the winter of 1922 addressed to the executives of the departments or to the Secretary of State of the various commonwealths in which the legislature sat, where the session laws are not yet available.

Three states still have no central authority.[24] Eleven[25] still have unpaid supervisory boards; ten[26] have administrative boards that are either unpaid or ex-officio; ten[27] have salaried boards of control; four[28] maintain two (or more) separate boards, one mainly supervisory, one mainly administrative; ten have created departments, eight under the general name of public welfare.[29]

Other features beside the general character of the authority are of interest. It will, however, not pay to review the whole field from these other points of view. A number of states[30] recognize the principle of geographic representation in the selection of the members of the board; many now require the presence of a woman or of several

---

[24] Mississippi, Nevada, Utah (which has had a Commission of Inquiry for two years).

[25] Colorado, Delaware, Georgia, Indiana, Louisiana, Maine, Maryland, Montana, New Hampshire, New York, North Carolina.

[26] Connecticut, Florida, Kentucky, Oregon, Rhode Island, South Carolina, Tennessee, Vermont, Virginia, Wyoming. Connecticut and Virginia are included here, although their boards have been in each case given the name Department of Public Welfare, since in each case the change of name carried no change in relationship to other branches of the government and in the case of Virginia no change in character or function. See, for similar change in the local field, the Massachusetts act changing the name of Boston Overseers of the Poor to Boston Commissioners of Public Welfare, without altering the character, powers or duties of those officials (Laws of 1921, chap. 146).

[27] Alabama (Control and Economy), Arizona (Board of Directors of State Institutions and Purchasing Agent), Iowa, Kansas, North Dakota, Oklahoma, South Dakota, Texas, West Virginia, Wisconsin.

[28] Arkansas (really three as there is an honorary board for the administration of the penitentiary), California (where there is the State Board of Charities, the Department of Institutions and a Board of Finance), Minnesota, Missouri (a State Board of Charities, a Board of Managers of Eleemosynary Institutions and a Department of Penal Institutions).

[29] Idaho, Illinois, Massachusetts, Michigan, Nebraska (without either abolishing or absorbing the Board of Control), New Jersey, New Mexico (really a Department of Health without responsibility for the charitable or penal institutions of the state), Ohio, Pennsylvania and Washington (Department of Business Control).

[30] E.g., Delaware, Florida, Kentucky, New York.

women;[31] several require the presence of certain types of experts.

Perhaps the most interesting considerations suggesting themselves in connection with the development of departmental schemes of organization, are those of the attempted creation of one agency within which shall be combined the advantages of supervision and of control. Under the Illinois departmental organization, for example, an attempt was made to retain the value of the critical and supervisory service so emphasized in the older days and between 1910 and 1917 embodied in the State Charities Commission, coördinate with the State Board of Administration. Under the departmental plan, there is a director at the head. Under him are a group of salaried executives, superintendents respectively of charities, of prisons and of parole, and an alienist and a criminologist. Under the director, also, is an unpaid Board of Public Welfare Commissioners, whose duties are to make investigations and to offer recommendations to the members of the department, or to the Governor or to the General Assembly on the request of those officials or on the initiative of the commission itself.[32] The members of the board as well as the executive

---

[31] The requirement concerning women represents political consideration for a large newly enfranchised group, and also recognizes the woman's assumed peculiar intelligence concerning the domestic problems involved in institutional management and concerning child care.

[32] Illinois Revised Statutes, 1919, chap. 24½, sections 3, 5, 8, 16, 25, 36, 37, 39.

members of the department are appointed by the
Governor and Senate and thus draw their authority from the same source. It is to be noted,
however, that the responsibility for making rules
for the conduct of the department, for laying before the Governor the needs of the department,
for making estimates and assignment of appropriations within the department rests with the director, while the Department of Finance, the first
named in the list of departments, is given authority to examine at all times the accuracy and
legality of accounts, receipts and expenditures
of the various departments. The disadvantage
under which the board suffers at any moment of
serious question or difference of view is obvious.
No special slur was therefore cast on the board
when after three years in office the first director
of the department assembled a committee of social
workers from all over the state, instead of making
use of the board created for this purpose, saying
that he did not know what should be done in the
field of child welfare and should like advice on the
point![33] The Massachusetts authority had, from
the first, been vested with certain administrative
functions, and, under the law of 1919,[34] the commissioner, who is head of the department, is appointed by the Governor and Senate for a term of
not more than five years as the executive and ad-

---

[33] *Report of the Illinois Department of Public Welfare,* Children's Committee, December, 1920.
[34] Acts of 1919, chap. 350, sec. 88.

ministrative head. He is, however, given a revolving board[35] of six unpaid members appointed
for terms of three years. This board is authorized
"to assist the commissioner . . . to keep informed of the public interests with which the department is charged, to study and investigate
questions arising in connection herewith, to consider, formulate and recommend proposals, to
advise with the Commissioner concerning policies.
. . ." It is clear, however, that the board, being
advisory to the commissioner and having no independent provision for making studies or for investigation on a wider scale than by individual
observation and conference, will probably find
itself limited to advising at the request of the commissioner, who may be so delayed in acquainting
himself with the problems of his department that
he finds difficulty in knowing just when to ask
for counsel.

The New Jersey Department of Institutions
and Agencies[36] has at its head a State Board of
Control of Agencies and Institutions[37] (the governor and eight appointed members, one a woman,
serving without pay in revolving terms of eight
years), which appoints the commissioner, who
although appointed by the board is described as

---

[35] Two of these must be women. *See* section 90.

[36] Created in 1918 under the name Department of Charities and Corrections, Laws of 1918, chap. 147, and given in 1919 its present name. Laws
of 1919, chap. 97.

[37] Styled under the Act of 1918 the State Board of Charities and
Correction.

being one of the two component elements of the department,[38] the board being the other.

An interesting question is that relating to the scope of the work of the department. In this is involved the question of relationship to other branches of the state government as well as that of relationships within the department. The early boards had to do with "charities and corrections." "Charities" meant paupers, lunatics, idiots, possibly the physically handicapped—blind, deaf and crippled; "Corrections" meant chiefly prisoners in jails and lock-ups. But paupers were often sick, and lunatics being non-able-bodied were often cared for as paupers, and prisoners were mostly poor. And the misery of all the groups therefore showed itself in the form of destitution.[39] When so many maladies had the same outward manifestation it was natural to place them all under one category. It was also inevitable that progressive analysis would lead to the multiplication of special and often of preventive service. Three fields of work were therefore recognized in the second incarnation of the Massachusetts authority,[40] but, in 1919, when it has been given the most general name by which it has ever been known, it occupies the most specialized field it has ever occupied and

---

[38] Laws of 1919, chap. 97, sec. 2.

[39] It is interesting to note that, when the commissioners of a few state boards assembled in 1872 and proposed a program to be presented to a larger gathering, all the items had to do with the field in "corrections." *Proceedings Ninth Annual Conference Charities and Corrections*, p. 11 (1882).

[40] When it became the Board of Health, Lunacy and Charity.

covers in fact only the problems of destitution and of child-care.[41] The department in Illinois, which prior to 1917 included only what might be called the mental diseases, destitution, and child welfare aspects of the problem, now is given the correctional agencies as well, and is vested with full governmental power. The department in Pennsylvania continues under its new title and new organization the lines of demarcation between relative emphasis on supervision and suggestion for other groups of wards and relative emphasis on administration in the case of lunatics, which were before expressed in a supervisory board of ten, one a lawyer and one a doctor, each of ten years' experience, to cover the whole field, while the two with professional experience with three others, selected by the board, were given their own executive and created a Committee on Lunacy with executive powers. Under the new situation, the department may create four bureaus, but one of them must be a Bureau of Lunacy. The functions ascribed to the new department in Idaho are those of a health authority, and in New Mexico, the department has health and child welfare functions.

One of the considerations moving those who advocated the advisory as distinguished from the

[41] For the time the work of the Homestead Commission seems submerged. It is to be noted, however, that a Commission on State Administration and Expenditures, in 1922, proposes a reconsolidation of the departments of health, corrections and mental diseases, and the institutional activities of the Department of Health with the Department of Public Welfare. Massachusetts House Document, No. 800. January, 1922, p. 22.

executive authority, was the fear of losing the
benefits of local initiative and of personal intimate
contacts, possible under local boards of management. The relationship worked out in Wisconsin
in the care of the insane represents a coöperation
between the central and the county authority.[42]
Under this plan, county institutions are established and utilized for certain groups of state
patients, the Board of Control, approving in advance the establishment and the plans proposed,
approving the bills before making the per capita
payments and retaining the power to remove a
patient whose care is unsatisfactory.   Under the
New Jersey act of 1918,[43] amended in 1919, creating the department of institutions and agencies,
the board appoints the boards of trustees of the
institutions and of the non-institutional agencies,
who in turn, appoint the chief executive of the
institution or agency (except the principal keeper
of the State Prison, who is a constitutional officer).   The chief executive, with the approval of
the board appointing him, selects the members of
his staff. The New Jersey Scheme is interesting
because, with the attempt to maintain and retain
the interests of members of boards, there is also
the attempt to secure for all institutions and all
agencies the benefit of expert services, and the
creation of Divisions of Medicine and Psychiatry,

[42] Hurd, *Institutional Care of the Insane,* I: chap. VI.
[43] Laws of New Jersey, 1918, chap. 147, Sections 112, 115; 1919, chap. 97.

of Labor and Agriculture, of Statistics, of Parole and of Dietetics, is also authorized.

Brief reference may also be made to two other problems. As was said in the opening paragraph, the issue between *wards* and *services* as a basis for allocating functions is often not clear-cut. Sometimes, however, the problem becomes an acute one. In the matter of the deaf and of the blind, there is frequently a sharp division of opinion as to the authority with which they should be associated, and there are found, therefore, not only great varieties of practice as between different states but frequent changes of practice within the same state. In some states, these groups are under special authorities, sometimes they are under public welfare, sometimes under education, sometimes under both education and public welfare.[44] In Massachusetts, Mothers' Aid administration is under public welfare; in Illinois, it is judicial; in Pennsylvania, the State Director reports to the State Education authority. Moreover, in Illinois, judicial administration is purely local; in Pennsylvania, the State Agent stimulates the organization of local commissions; in Massachusetts, the Overseers of the Poor (local) administer, subject to the advice and counsel of the state department, and, if the department approves,

---

[44] Best, *The Deaf, Their Position in Society and the Provision for Their Education in the United States* (1914): also, *The Blind, Their Condition and the Work Being Done for them* (1919). The same discussion occurs in the case of schools for dependent children.

the local work recovers one-third of the cost from the state treasury for the locality.

The second problem to which brief reference might be made is that of coöperation among the various departments which have a common interest in the same services or in the same wards. Under the Illinois statute it is provided that the directors are to devise methods of coöperating and to secure the coördination of the work of the various departments. . . .[45] Since there are great experiments in departmental coöperation being worked out on a national scale under the so-called Smith-Lever act, the Smith-Hughes act and the Sheppard-Towner act, in fields nearly related to that of "public welfare," it is unnecessary, perhaps, to do more than call attention to the need of developing a fine art of coöperation[46] among the agencies concerned with common undertakings.

To review briefly—after sixty years of effort, there are still commonwealths that have taken no step in the direction of organizing their service in this general field on a state-wide basis: there are eight that recognize the field as one of a greater or smaller number of fields to which are devoted special departmental organizations. Those eight and the other thirty-seven that have taken some action in this direction show diversity at well-nigh

[45] Illinois Revised Statutes, chap. 24½, sec. 26.
[46] One feels hesitant to use the word "coöperation" which, like "charities" and "homes" and various other beautiful and significant terms, has been first used, then abused and then discarded!

every point, and manifest variations accounted for by differences not only in need, situation, character of work to be done, but by variations due also to inertia, to lack of agreement on certain fundamental principles of effective governmental action and in part, undoubtedly, to lack of such authoritative leadership as might come from a national service soundly developed and based on the fundamental demand that the victims of social and economic maladjustment be adequately cared for, the symptoms traced to their source, and the wisdom acquired from sound treatment and thorough analysis applied to constructive and preventive attacks upon the social and economic ills thus revealed.

CHAPTER III

FORM, FUNCTIONS, OBJECTIVES, AND ORGANIZATION

K EEPING in mind the facts relating to the historical development and wide variation found in the several states as outlined in Chapter 2, it is important to examine a summary of the various types of state systems for the purpose of studying and illustrating present practices. We shall examine, therefore, charts showing prevalent forms and additional features as found in state agencies and state systems with later a separate statement concerning the varied and complex functions of such agencies. The methods of classification and description vary according to differences in form, differences in function, differences in objects of public welfare, and differences in degree of centralization. It will be clear to the reader that such a simple and inadequate scheme will serve only to crystallize the discussions of public welfare systems about some of the salient and common features of public welfare. It will be clear further that these graphic representations are no more than norms or types and that actual agencies depart from the norms in numerous details.

FORM OF ORGANIZATION

There are three prevalent types of state agency as fixed by constitution and form and a fourth miscellaneous group susceptible to an additional amount of classification.   The four groups are:

The Departmental Form.
The Professional Board Form.
The Lay Board Form.
Miscellaneous Forms.

The Department.   The term "department" is commonly applied to many different divisions of government.   It is used in a restricted sense here, and applies to any division headed by a single official appointed by the governor.   Officials so appointed may have relations to the governor analogous to relations enjoyed by cabinet officials toward the President.   The term includes, however, not only those larger divisions of government managed by very important officials, but any divisions which are similarly constituted and organized.   There are large and small divisions of this type all through the field of public welfare in the United States.   Several state governments are operated exclusively on the departmental plan, although in most states isolated departments here and there perform limited services of one kind or another.   Examples of both situations appear in the materials of the following chapters.

The department has certain rather exclusive characteristics.   It is, as stated, headed by a single directing officer chosen by the governor and approved by the legislature (usually, the senate only endorses the appointment). The officer is most often designated "Director," "Commissioner," or "Secretary." He has direct responsibility to the Governor who may sometimes and under certain conditions divest him of control of departmental services. His salary varies from $4,000 to $10,-000 annually, and his tenure from "the pleasure of the governor" to definite periods of four or five years. Certain checks apply to his authority, and these may chiefly be of two kinds. The general oversight of the governor, by virtue of his selection of the chief, may be extended to apply also to subordinate bureau heads. If he does not appoint the latter, he may be empowered to endorse their selection, and sometimes even the selection of a considerable number of the rank and file of employees. This extends the governor's authority and power into the details of public welfare administration. In a second respect, the chief of the department may be "supervised" by an "advisory board," or "Board of Welfare Commissioners" as it is called in Illinois. When such board exists, it is usually appointed by the governor, the same as the department chief, with the consent of the senate. It may supervise departmental activities and consult with the chief. It often has legislative and judicial functions associated with those activities. It may approve appointments within the department, and so on. In fact, it may have very substantial powers as the

boards of the Massachusetts departments appear
to have; or it may be a fairly innocuous appendage
of the department, as happens in Illinois.[1] In the
case of California, advisory boards have been
created from the several one-time boards of trustees of state institutions, which have been shorn
of all but advisory functions, and now coöperate
with the "Department of Institutions" in the management of their respective institutions. Other
advisory boards not related to departments are
considered in the miscellaneous group of agencies.

Thus the state department, with its chief executive appointed by the governor and vested in some
cases with very wide powers, checked on the one
hand by the governor's authority, and on the
other, perhaps, by some form of "advisory board"
appointed by the governor, is a feature of organization in much public welfare work by the states.
A brief evaluation of the form may be helpful.
Departments have increased in number greatly
since the war, and may, in measure, be an expression of war needs. Efficiency in the management
of government is sought through a hierarchy of
control culminating in the chief executive. Although greater official responsibility is thought to
derive from this relatively simple scheme, it seems,
compared with other plans, to expose welfare
work under it to two dangers. First, the responsi-

---

[1] The Illinois legislature failed to make appropriations for the "Board of
Welfare Commissioners" several years ago, and the board has since become
inactive.

LEGEND CHARTS

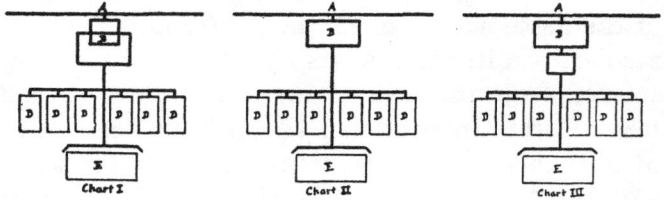

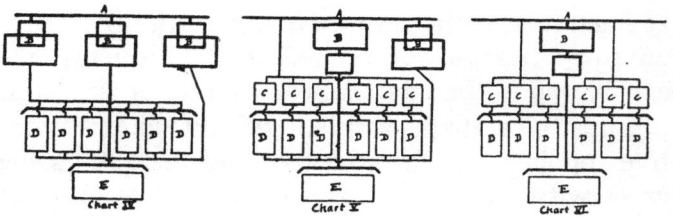

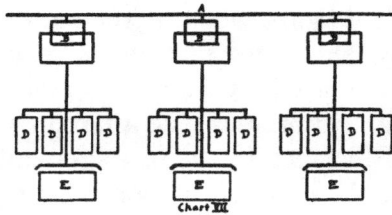

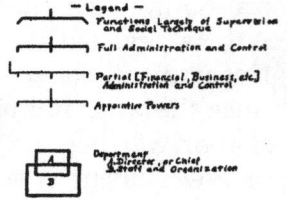

- Organization -

Chart I   State Department
Chart II   Professional Board
Chart III Lay Board
Chart IV   Departments "Modally" Specialized
Chart V   Modal Specialization and Partial Decentralization
Chart VI   Social Technique Centralized, Other Functions Decentralized
Chart VII Specialization on the Basis of "Scope"

A   Appointing Authority, Generally "Governor and Senate"
B   Centralized State Agencies
C   Decentralized State Agencies

- Legend -

Functions Largely of Supervision and Social Technique

Full Administration and Control

Partial [Financial, Business, etc.] Administration and Control

Appointive Powers

Department
A. Director, or Chief
B. Staff and Organization

Professional Board

Lay Board
A. The Board
B. Executive Secretary and Staff.

D   State Institutions
E   General and Local Functions

bility implied is political, and thus a peculiar responsibility. Second, executive action, however commendable, is apt to be confined to the more settled practices of existing official precedent. At any rate, the nature of official responsibility, of itself, does not seem wholly favorable to a close rapport with all the legitimate interests of the state and its several communities. "Advisory Boards" may be attached to departments to meet both the difficulties above suggested. Whether the difficulties are thus adequately met is a question of how paramount they are thought to be. Affecting the nature of the department itself, the principle of ascending responsibility upon which it is chiefly based is modified in practice when the governor has extensive direct powers within the department. To the degree, also, that the advisory boards become functionally significant, in operation, the type assumes more the character of the "lay board" form which will be treated a little later.

The departmental form is illustrated in Chart I. This shows a single agency and not a state system. Where departments are the rule, welfare work is most often split functionally among several of them. State systems of this kind are illustrated in Charts IV and VII.

The Professional Board. This is usually a small board of three to five members appointed by the governor with the consent of the legislature.

The members all receive salaries, which amount in the most important cases to from $3000 to $5000; and then devote full time to official duties. While the board occupies a position analagous to that of department chief, exercising similar functions for the most part, its plural-headedness makes it a different type of executive. The members are sometimes made individually responsible for specific duties within the organization, working perhaps, as bureau chiefs, and acting in concert over matters related to general policy, rules of procedure, and needs of coöperation. The "Board of Control" in California is so organized. In general, however, no specific duties are allotted to individual members, the board as a whole being responsible for partitioning services. Tenure of the members is fixed for specified periods of time, but the governor frequently has the power of removal for cause, and under set conditions. The board by nature is relatively autonomous, due to its plural composition, the manner of rotating appointments, and the fixed tenure of its membership. Terms of office are long, and expire at different times, so that an entire board is seldom constituted by a single governor during one term of office, or at least not all at one time. Abrupt changes in the services controlled by such a board do not, therefore, often occur. Autonomy varies a little, however, with local conditions. If the governor is ex officio member and president of the

board, or if the board acts on important matters
only, "with the consent of the governor," both of
which conditions occur, its autonomy is limited.
On the whole, however, the nature of the board is
favorable to stability of policy and service. The
principle of overlapping terms possible only with
a board is exceedingly valuable in actual practice.
Experience in Illinois at the time the board system was replaced by departmental organization in
all branches of government, is instructive in this
particular.[2] The apparent efficiency of boards in
neighboring states is also instructive.[3]

Qualifications for membership on these boards
is not uniformly stipulated in legislation. The law
sometimes provides that members shall be selected
equally from opposing political parties, as nearly
as possible; sometimes that there shall be one or
more women members; sometimes that they shall
be electors; etc. Large discretion rests with the
appointing authority. The payment of substantial
salaries and the nature of employment seem to imply the intent to get competent, specially qualified
officials for the positions. Technical qualifications, however, are very rare of mention. Standards of professional fitness applied to the office,
intangible as are such as exist in welfare work,
seem, in practice, to be most often standards of

------

[2] Wright, Henry C. "A Valuation of a System for the Administration of
State Institutions Through One Man Control As Operated in Illinois."
State Charities Aid Association Publication, 1922, p. 47.
[3] Especially the Boards of Minnesota and Wisconsin.

other established services (financial, business, legal, etc.).

Thus the character of this form of board, and of the functions often allotted to it, seem to imply that it is chiefly an executive board. Payment of salaries, professional implications in the office, small size of the board, and sometimes the antecedent historical conditions back of the original creation of many of these boards, suggest such a conclusion. The form thus embodies the desire to secure efficient service for the state through the provision, and protection in office, of experts, rather than through the system of linear responsibility previously described. The values of such organization and constitution thus partially depend upon whether a council of administrative officials, however expert, may properly supervise their own acts, and sufficiently unite their services to the rather extensive social interests of the state. Examples of the professional board were cited above.[4] Others are listed in the following chapters. The form is illustrated in Chart II.

The Lay Board. The constitution of the lay board is similar to that of the professional board. It is usually a little larger, having five to twelve members, with an average of about seven. Its members are appointed for definite terms which vary in the more important cases from three to

---

[4] Previous citation.

eight years, but average five or six.[5] Qualifications for membership are substantially those cited
for the other form of board. In about half the
cases, the purpose of the law is to secure a non-
partisan board; and in about half, women are included among membership. Overlapping terms of
office effect the same continuity of function possible for professional boards. It is provided in case
of the New York "State Board of Charities" that
members shall represent districts of the state. In
Delaware and many of the southern states this
provision may apply to all forms of board. In
general, this form differs little in the foregoing
respects from the professional board, except that
it is larger, and implications that it be a representative body seem a little more obvious. Some
striking differences appear, however. No salaries
are paid to members on this form of board. They
are limited to compensation for expenses while attending to official duties. In New York and
Maine a small "per diem" is paid; and a nominal
salary of one to one hundred dollars per year is
allowed in a few other cases; but even these are
exceptional. The members cannot, therefore, devote full time to the office. Professional services
are not commanded, in any sense of the word, by
the salaries paid.

Another distinguishing feature of this organization is that the board must be served by an

[5] Members of the "Board of Prison Directors" in California serve for ten years.

executive officer,[6] usually called "secretary" or
"commissioner." He is employed by the board
much as a manager is employed by any board of
directors, or a superintendent is employed by a
school board. He is presumably a qualified individual, (an expert, who receives adequate compensation, fixed within limits by the board,) and
is responsible for directing the details of the welfare work. In so doing he exercises, for the most
part, functions delegated by the board, and is
supervised by the board in the exercise of those
functions. Administration is thus differentiated,
—executive functions fall to the lot of a professional employee, while deliberative functions are
reserved for a lay board. Responsibility of salaried officials is confined to authority within the
field of public welfare, and thus may be freed
from the censure of extraneous services and affili-
ations. The superposition of a board between the
appointing authority of the state and the administration of technical services, is the distinguishing
feature of the organization under consideration.
Of course the principle is not clearly expressed in
practice. The matter of allocating the different
functions is seldom the subject of legislation. All
are simply vested in the board. Where allotments
are made, more often than not violence has been
done to the real values of the principle. New

---

[6] Boards too small to afford one are put in the "Miscellaneous" classification. The executive must be more than a mere clerk, or recording officer.

Hampshire, Connecticut,[7] and Kentucky are states where it has notably been attempted. The principle of division of function, valuable as it may prove to be, should receive more intelligent treatment in state laws. Quite likely, it will be increasingly recognized and applied in future legislation.

Some of the advantages thought to reside in lay board organization may be summed up as follows: (1) Superposition of a board between the appointing authority of the state (the governor) and the active administrators of the service in question tends to confine immediate responsibility for the conduct of that service to agencies non-political in kind, and associated solely and primarily with the field of public welfare itself. (2) The board, by the manner of its construction, is a stabilizing factor in the service, and protects its integrity as a service. (3) Expertness of qualification may be defined by the board in terms suited to the nature of the work, and to the availability of qualified persons in it. (4) The opportunity is present for full expression of welfare activities (within legal limits) as peculiar values of the state service, not to be submerged in traditional functions of government, or the standards of other services. (5) Explicit provision is made for the organization of lay (democratic) interests as well as the accepted official (more autocratic) functions in welfare. (6) The work is thus on a broad social foundation.

---

[7] There are two executives under one board in Connecticut, directing the field between them.

The board, retaining ultimate responsibility for all policies and their effects, is available through its members to interpret the work to the people in the communities of the state and seek their intelligent participation in its program. Under favorable conditions, the work is based upon a close liaison with community enterprises along welfare lines.

Lay boards have prominent functions in many states. They are called "Board of Public Welfare," "Board of Charities and Corrections," "Board of Control," and even "Department of Public Welfare." The type is illustrated in Chart III. Systems of which this form is a part are illustrated in Charts V and VI. Other illustrations appear in the following chapters.

Miscellaneous Forms. This includes a large variety of agency not quite "normal" to any of the three forms described. This may be due either to manner of constitution or to peculiarity of function. The commonest method of constituting the various miscellaneous agencies is by ex-officio membership. In fact a few boards, quite similar in function and organization to one or other of the types considered, differ only in this one respect from them. State officers, usually taken from among the governor, secretary of state, attorney general, treasurer, comptroller, superintendent of public instruction, chief health officer, architect, engineer, or other department heads, are assembled into a "board," "commission," or "cabinet" and invested with welfare powers. For the government of major service departments, such as a public welfare department, the exclusive use of this method of constituting governing boards is rare. The method is applied to constitute institutional boards of management in some of the southern and western states. Its most prevalent uses, indeed, are associated with control of state institutions. It is frequently applied to form agencies for limited or temporary purposes of various kinds; and the principle involved is present, of course, in a governor's "cabinet," which is the advisory body resulting from the organization of state government into departments, exclusively.

In certain cases ex-officio membership is mixed with other types of membership on boards. It is used, apparently, to secure coöperation and integration of services between government departments. On several of the lay or professional boards of the country, for instance, the governor is ex officio member of the board, and may be chairman. In one state the secretary of the state board of health serves on the welfare board, ex officio; in another, an advisory board consists of the commissioner of health, commissioner of labor, commissioner of public welfare, ex officio, and several lay members; etc.

The governor's "council" or "cabinet" of state officers may, among other things, have official veto

over the acts of the several departments. Such a
body, ostensibly, serves to unite state services
which are severed, by organization, into independent units. The "State Administrative Board" in
Michigan is one example of the type, and the various "councils" of the New England States may be
considered others. Where a tight organization
like the council has not occurred, certain state officers nevertheless have important relations to
welfare work, and exercise increasingly powerful
functions as the elements of that work become less
concretely organized. In New York, for example,
the "comptroller" has duties which are assigned,
in states where the total system is simpler, to the
state boards, or departments actually responsible
for welfare work. The "Supervisor of Administration" in Massachusetts is a more recent
example of a general officer supervising certain
aspects of the several state services. General state
officials, whether organized into bodies, or as individuals, necessarily have close relations to the
branches of government; the degree or kind of
relationships involved seem to have a great deal
to do with the relative autonomy of the departments, and the integrity of their several services.

Still another important type of ex-officio agency
is one designed to secure coöperation between departments without exercising superior or arbitrary
control over them; yet different from the mixed
membership scheme already considered. Perhaps

the most remarkable example is the semi-official committee known as the "Commonwealth Committee" of Pennsylvania. It unites several departments through a common but distinct organization. With the extension of this organization into local communities, Pennsylvania has become unique in its practical effort to solve the difficulties of coöperation.

A great number of lesser agencies may be only hastily surveyed here. A random sampling of them would include parole boards, probation commissions, childrens' code commissions, lesser advisory boards, and such specific agencies as the "Board of Women Visitors" of Minnesota, the "Hospital Development Commission" of New York, the "Advisory Commission for State Sanatoria" of Minnesota, the "Legislative Visiting Committee" of Wisconsin, the "Salary Classification Commission" of New York, the "Poor Law Commission" of Pennsylvania, etc. Such boards and commissions are extremely varied in character. They may be of limited duration; may have very small powers; may exercise functions only intermittently; may be sporadic creations of the legislature or may be essential parts of a larger state scheme of organization. A loosely knit state system, such as that in New York, is apt to possess many of them; while a newly, or closely organized state system utilizes few, if any, such agencies. There are a number of public welfare officials elected by popular vote. The "Prison Commission" of Georgia, the "Trustees of the State Prison" in Mississippi, and the Commissioner of Public Welfare" in Oklahoma are so chosen.

DISTRIBUTION OF FUNCTIONS

There are three types of function described by this second classification of state agencies. The functions are here called, collectively:

Financial Administration,
Business Administration,
Administration of Social Work.

Financial Administration. Functions under this head are the familiar ones of paying bills, auditing accounts, prescribing methods of book-keeping, authorizing disbursements and expenditures, supervising budgets, having custody of public funds, and many others like them. When financial matters are separated from welfare services, they are vested in such agencies as departments of finance, state boards of accounts, the treasurer, comptroller, etc. These agencies, then, are not peculiar to welfare, but act for all the state services demanding work of financial character.[8] Some general state boards of control, and many smaller boards of control for state institutions combine financial and business routine in their

---

[8] Examples are: "Board of Control" in California; "Department of Finance" in Illinois; "State Board of Accounts" in Indiana; "Superintendent of Purchase" in New York; etc.

work. Where such extension of authority from
the financial field into general business administration occurs, there is also more apt to be a limitation in the scope of the authority thus exercised
to matters associated with physical properties, and
usually strictly to welfare work itself.

Business Administration. Functions here involved apply to the management of the physical
assets of welfare work, and also to the management of the work's personnel. Such functions
most characteristically relate to the management
of state institutions. They may include the purchase of supplies and equipment, the construction
and maintenance of buildings, the custody of
state property, and other matters of management
of properties. Applied to persons, they involve
the hiring, pay, and supervision of employees, and
the government of state wards.[9]

Administration of Social Work. The meaning
of social work has been growing within the past
fifty years. Associated with state government, its
peculiar merits were not appreciated until a shift
in the *locus* of that work as it used to be, was accomplished. Social work no longer attends chiefly
to the confinement and management of state
wards, but derives its problems from community
processes far beyond state institutions. With the
change in orientation, there has come a corre-

---

[9] Examples are: "Department of Institutions" in California; "Depart-
ment of Business Administration" in Washington; "Department of Public
Works and Buildings" in Illinois; "Superintendent of State's Prisons" in
New York; etc.

sponding change in the nature of social work. It ceases to be spoken of exclusively in terms of supervision over established government services which are chiefly institutional in character, and becomes important as administration of community services. Thus social work is a constructive administrative enterprise of increasing magnitude. On account of the necessary reference to social ends involved in social work thus broadly conceived, those ends must be fixed through appreciation of the social processes themselves in any state, and their merits defined in terms of social values. Hence the need of integrating this work with modern community life. Yet a critical problem in the administration of social work is precisely the problem of values. Who determines values, and how is it done? Is public welfare a state function exclusively or is it essentially a matter of local responsibility when the matter of values is decided? The question finally becomes one of organization for the welfare agencies of the state because these values are appreciably involved in organization. Is any given type of agency which administers social work more sensitive to community processes than any other? Is the responsibility of the service, as fixed by organization, socially or autocratically minded? Perhaps it is a question of democracy, and is important for the future direction of welfare work as a state function.

If a split in functions of welfare along the lines here discussed is the feature of any state system, then more than one agency is necessary to administer the service as a whole. Agencies for the special parts of it, business, finance, or social work, may be of any form whatever, and may differ in form among themselves. They may be, one and all, major state departments, or some of them may be minor organizations. Functions may be united so that one, two, or three agencies exist to share them; while in rare cases one type of service may be omitted. (Social work appears to have been overlooked in the schemes of organization of Washington and Tennessee to the degree that it is almost an omission.) Charts IV, V, and VI all illustrate state systems variously organized on the bases of differences in assignment of functions.

DIFFERENCES IN OBJECT

Since our definition of public welfare was derived from a composite picture of functions existing for extensively developed systems of public welfare, it is possible to compare states with respect to differences in the total extent of the field which they have adopted for their work. Such a comparison would not meet an immediate organization problem, however, and is aside from the purposes of this chapter. Sometimes, however, there is a division of function within state boundaries and between state agencies which is

determined by the various special objects of the
welfare service (criminals, defectives, children,
state wards, etc.). This, then, becomes of interest
as a problem of the organization of a state system.
The clearest example of a systematic distinction
in the objects of a state service as the basis of
organization is found in Massachusetts.[10]   Other
examples of such distinction are numerous, but
not so evidently planned as this.   Essentially the
same distinctions occur in New York, but with
numerous other complications in organization to
obscure them.   There is little real consensus in
practice as to which objects should be classed together, and which separated (if any) for the
purpose of gross organization of welfare administration.   In two of the states institutional management is entirely severed from all relationships
with other welfare work.   Elsewhere prison administration is frequently so separated.   Negro
welfare may be separately provided for.   Child
welfare and probation are often special objects of
organization, etc.   In few cases apparently do
these splits in organization reflect systematic planning for the whole; and they may be evidences
of a rather rapid, planless increase in the field of
welfare work.   Certain peculiarities in some of
the highly organized systems which have resulted

---

[10] Massachusetts has provided the following state departments, all of which
exercise some more or less customary welfare functions: (1) "Department
of Public Welfare"; (2) "Department of Health"; (3) "Department of Corrections"; (4) "Department of Mental Deficiency"; (5) "Probation Commission."

from reorganizations present apparent compromises between the former condition of scattered organization and the desire for better direction of effort. The total effect in some cases may conceivably be too much organization.[11]

Chart VII illustrates organization divided by particular objects of service. The agencies constituting such a system may be of any form and any degree of importance whatever.

CENTRALIZATION OF STATE ORGANIZATION

Specific attention need be given here to only the lesser agencies which enter into any state system. The governor, or the governor's cabinet may be a focus of course, for all state services. Each of the services may in turn be focussed in a central state department, headed by a single chief or a board. On the other hand, there may be a series of small boards or officials severally responsible to no single body within the field of public welfare. Public welfare in the states is served by systems described as anywhere between the former and the latter conditions. Several states have little or no central system at all, yet have many agencies, while others have highly organized systems, yet only one agency that is important. Reorganization, however, may abolish the lesser forms, or may assimilate them without abolishing them. The

---

[11] See, in this connection, state organizations in Connecticut, New Jersey and Michigan.

important thing to notice in this connection is, that everywhere the service of welfare appears to have grown most by multiplying agencies to perform particular services, and then by a subsequent reorganization, having them all modified in accordance with a plan. In such modifications the small agencies, many of them, disappear, yet certain of them persist. It would be useful to know if there is any common law which selects those to persist. It is only possible to point out that some which have persisted seem to have certain functional values. The type which often survives is that type known as trustees, or board of control of state institutions. There is no form of lesser board which has not been assimilated into state departments recently organized, yet in several cases boards of trustees have survived with attenuated powers, or with functions closely integrated with the larger state system. Such boards exist in California and New Jersey. It seems possible that some of the smaller agencies, such as these boards, are valuable instruments for the embodiment of disinterested public service for the state through laymen who are closely associated with the communities these institutions serve. There is a similar suggestion of the value of services by laymen in the relations which seem to exist between institutional boards and the larger state systems in such places as Indiana and North Carolina. Without assuming too much on the basis of limited data, it appears that the lesser state agencies might be classified into those having local significance and those having no specific local significance, and an effort made in future organization or reorganization of state systems to salvage all values which exist in the organization problem relevant to the marshalling of every kind of significant lay and private interest in public welfare work.

Wherever agencies are organized into a system some scheme of subordination and superordination is necessary. Variations in the practice are represented in systems such as have already been cited, and in much of the materials of the following chapters. Charts V and VI show types of state systems with different degrees of centralization.

It is perhaps too much to expect to be able to present an adequate view of state systems *in general* in the United States, in such brief space. Certain it is that a proper evaluation of the systems would be too much. This general study, however, has developed certain features of state welfare work as now organized which appear to be significant for the whole movement. Those experienced with these features may best supply the judgments necessary for evaluation.

To sum up briefly, general features of state systems have been presented through analyses of state agencies for public welfare. The agencies have been classified according to those features which seem significant for an understanding of their respective characters and merits. The classifications were fourfold in kind, and within each kind there were types selected for detailed analysis. The study was therefore organized about the following topics: (1) *Differences in form,* including (a) departments, (b) professional boards, (c) lay boards, and (d) miscellaneous forms. (2) *Differences in distribution of functions,* including the differences between the technical services of (a) administration of finance, (b) administration of business affairs, and (c) administration of social work. (3) *Differences in objects of public welfare.* (4) *Differences in degree of centralized organization* of the systems. Further analysis of form may better be done in connection with the study of particular state systems.

CHAPTER IV

THE RANGE OF STATE AGENCIES

THE information presented in chapter 3, dealing largely with organization and function, represented a sort of total or aggregate summary of prevailing state systems. Important alongside this summary is the range of names or classifications of the different state agencies in accordance with their distribution by states. This list is representative of the number and variety existing in the United States and the classification follows the general divisions set forth in the previous chapter. This classification included five types of organization—*The Departmental Form* (a), *The Professional Board Form* (b), *The Lay Board Form* (c), *The Ex-officio Board Form* (d), and *The Mixed Organization Type* (b-d).

This chapter will attempt to present still another picture of the types or form of state authorities and agencies through which the student of public welfare may interpret the principle and practices as well as the patterns upon which new systems may be built and old systems revised. The most effective way to present this material is also the simplest way, namely, presentation, state by state, in their alphabetical order.

ALABAMA

Child Welfare Department (a)
State Board of Convict Supervisors
Board of Pardons (d)
Boards of Trustees for various institutions

ARIZONA

State Child Welfare Board (c)
Board of Pardons and Paroles (c)
Boards of Directors of state institutions (b-d)

ARKANSAS

State Purchasing Agent (a)
State Commission for the Blind (c)
State Board of Penitentiary Reform School (b)

CALIFORNIA

State Department of Public Welfare
Department of Institutions (a)
Board of Control (Finance Department) (b)
State Board of Prison Directors (c)
Advisory Pardon Board (c)
Advisory Boards for institutions managed by
the Department of Institutions (c)

COLORADO

Department of Charities and Corrections (a)
Colorado Board of Corrections (b)
Child Welfare Bureau (jointly supervised by
the Department of Public Instruction and the
Board of Control) (c)
Boards of Control for state institutions (c)

CONNECTICUT

Department of Public Welfare (c)
State Tuberculosis Commission (b)
Department of State Agencies and Institutions
(appointed by State Treasurer) (a)
State Board of Finance (d)
State Board of Control (d)
Board of Education for the Blind (c-d)
Boards of Trustees for state institutions
Connecticut Infirmary Commission (tempo-
rary)

DELAWARE

State Board of Charities (c)
Health and Welfare Commission (c)
Board of Parole (c)
Delaware Commission for the Blind (c)
Delaware Commission for the Feeble-Minded
(c)
Mothers' Pensions Commission (c)
State Child Labor Commission (c)
Board of State Supplies (b-d)
Boards of Trustees for combined state-local
institutions
Pardon Official (Lieut.-Gov.)

FLORIDA

Board of Commissioners of State Institutions
(d)
Pardon Board (d)
Board of Health (care of deaf and blind) (c)

GEORGIA

Board of Public Welfare (c)
Community Service Commission (c)
State Board of Health (care of tuberculous and mental defectives) (c)
Prison Commission (a paid, elective board)
Boards of Trustees for state institutions

IDAHO

Department of Public Welfare (and health) (a)
State Tuberculosis Commission (c)
Board of State Prison Commissioners (d)
State Board of Education (deaf, blind, and industrial schools) (c)

ILLINOIS

Department of Public Welfare (a) includes
    Board of Public Welfare Commissioners (c)
Department of Public Works and Buildings (a)
Department of Finance (a)

INDIANA

Board of State Charities (c)
State Board of Accounts (d)
Board of Industrial Aid for the Blind (c)
Board of Pardons (c)
Boards of Trustees for state institutions (b and c)

IOWA

State Board of Control (b)
State Board of Parole (c)

KANSAS

Board of Administration for State Institutions (b)
State Accountant (a)
State Architect (a)
Kansas Commission for the Blind (c-d)
Board of Managers for the Soldiers' Home (c)

KENTUCKY

State Board of Charities and Corrections (c)

LOUISIANA

Board of Charities and Corrections (c)
Board of Parole (c)
General Manager for the State's Prison (a)
State Board of Education (cares for deaf and blind) (c)
Boards of Managers for state institutions

MAINE

State Board of Charities and Corrections (c) (serve at $5.00 per diem)
Advisory Board of Parole (c)
Boards of Trustees for groups of state institutions, including
    Trustees of Juvenile Institutions
    Board of Prison Inspectors
    Trustees for Women's Reformatories
    Hospital Trustees
Governor and Council
State-local probation officers (a)

MARYLAND

Department of Charities (c)
Department of Welfare (a)
Board of Mental Hygiene (a-c)
Boards of Trustees for state institutions

MASSACHUSETTS

Department of Public Welfare (a) including
Advisory Board of Public Welfare (c)
Department of Mental Diseases (a) including
Advisory Commission on Mental Diseases (c)
Department of Health (a) including
The Public Health Council (c)
Department of Corrections (a) including
The Parole Board (b)
Probation Commission (c)
Boards of Trustees for state institutions in Department of Public Welfare and Department of Mental Diseases (b and c)

MICHIGAN

State Welfare Department (a) including
State Welfare Commission (c)
State Hospital Commission (c)
State Prison Commission (c)
State Corrections Commission (c)
State Institutions Commission (c)
State Administrative Board (d)

MINNESOTA

State Board of Control (b)
State Board of Parole (d)
Prison Labor Commission (c)
Board of Women Visitors (c)
Minnesota Advisory Commission for State
Sanitaria (c)

MISSISSIPPI

Pardoning Board (c)
Trustees of the Penitentiary (a paid, elective
board)
State Board of Health (for tuberculosis and
hospitals)
Boards of Trustees for a limited number of
state institutions

MISSOURI

State Board of Charities and Corrections (c)
Department of Penal Institutions (b)
Board of Managers of Eleemosynary Institu-
tions (a-c)
Commission for the Blind (c)

MONTANA

Board of Charities and Reform (c)
Bureau of Child and Animal Potection (c)
State Board of Pardons (d)
State Board of Health (for child welfare, juve-
nile defectives and delinquents) (c) includes
    Montana Orthopedic Commision (c)

State Purchasing Department (a)

State Parole Commissioner (a)

Governor, Secretary of State, and Attorney General comprising,

State Prison Commission

State Board of Examiners

Trustees for three state institutions

Boards of trustees for other state institutions (c-d)

NEVADA

Boards of trustees for state institutions including

Board of State Prison Commissioners (d)

Board of Trustees for the State Orphans' Home (d)

Board of Trustees for the State Institution for Delinquent Boys (c)

State Board of Pardons (d)

NEW HAMPSHIRE

State Board of Charities and Corrections (c)

Purchasing Agent (a)

Governor and Council

Boards of Trustees for state institutions (c-d)

NEW JERSEY

Department of Institutions and Agencies (a) including

Managing Boards of state institutions (c)

State Board of Children's Guardians (c)

NEW MEXICO

Public Welfare Department (including health) (c)
Girls' Welfare Board (c)
Boards of Trustees and Commissions for state institutions

NORTH CAROLINA

State Board of Charities and Public Welfare (c)
Advisory Board of Parole (d)
Child Welfare Commission (d)
Department of Public Instruction (adult defectives) (d)
Boards of Trustees for state institutions (c)

NEBRASKA

Department of Public Welfare (including health) (a)
Board of Control (b)
Department of Finance (a)
Board of Pardons (d)

NEW YORK

State Board of Charities (c)
Prison Commission (c)
Superintendent of State's Prisons (a)
Department of Purchase (a)
Commission for Mental Defectives (c)
Hospital Commission (b)
Probation Commission (c)

Parole Board (c-d)
Hospital Development Commission (d)
Department of Education (for deaf and blind)
Department of Health (for tuberculosis hospitals)
New York State Commission for the Blind (c)
Salary Classification Commission (d)
Board of Classification
Building Improvement Commission (d)
Child Welfare Commission (temporary)
Commission on New Prisons (temporary)
General state officers (Governor, Comptroller, Attorney General, Treasurer, etc.)
Boards of Managers of state institutions

NORTH DAKOTA
Board of Administration (b)
Board of Pardons (c-d)

OHIO
Department of Public Welfare (a) including
    Board of Pardons and Paroles (c)
    Ohio Commission for the Blind (c)
    (Advisory boards within the Department optional with the Director and the Governor)
Ohio Penitentiary Commission
Department of Finance (a)
Board of Trustees for Ohio Soldiers and Sailors Orphans Home

OKLAHOMA
State Board of Public Affairs (b)

Board of Prison Control (d)
Department of Charities and Corrections (Commissioner elective) (a)
Board of Pardons (d)
Children's Code Commission
Boards of Managers of state institutions (generally including education or health officers ex officio) (c-d)

OREGON

State Board of Control (d)
Child Welfare Commission (c)
Board of Parole (c-d)
Board of Child Labor ( )

PENNSYLVANIA

Department of Welfare (a) including
    State Welfare Commission (c)
    Boards of Trustees of state institutions (c)
Department of State Finances (a)
Department of Public Instruction (for deaf, dumb, and blind) (a)
Board of Pardons (d)
Department of Property and Supplies (a)
Penal Code Commission (temporary)
Children's Code Commission (temporary)
Poor Law Commission (temporary)
Commonwealth Committee

RHODE ISLAND

Penal and Charitable Commission (c)
Board of Parole (c)

Two Boards of Female Visitors (c)
Boards of Trustees for state institutions

SOUTH CAROLINA

State Board of Public Welfare (c)
Board of Pardons (c)
Committee on Deaf and Blind Children
Boards of Trustees for some of the state institutions

TENNESSEE

Department of Institutions (a)
Department of Finance (a)
Advisory Committee for the Soldiers' Home (c)

TEXAS

Board of Control (b)
Board of Prison Commissioners (b)
Board of Pardon Advisors (b)
Anti-tuberculosis Commission (c-d)
Boards of Trustees for some of the state institutions

UTAH

State Welfare Commission (c-d)
Boards of Trustees and Commissions for state institutions

VERMONT

Department of Public Welfare (a)
Department of Finance (a)
Trustees of Soldiers' Home (c)

VIRGINIA

State Department of Public Welfare (c)
Purchasing Commission, including
   Commissioner of State Hospitals (a)
Department of Education (for deaf and blind)
Boards of trustees for state institutions
Commission on Mental Defectives (d) (temporary)

WASHINGTON

Department of Business Control (a)
Department of Efficiency (a)
Administrative Board (d)
Two Parole Boards (c)

WEST VIRGINIA[1]

State Board of Control (b)
State Board of Children's Guardians (c)
Penitentiary Board of Directors
Bureau of Negro Welfare and Statistics (a)
Child Welfare Commission (temporary)

WISCONSIN

State Board of Control (b)
Memorial Hospital Commission (temporary)

WYOMING

State Board of Charities and Reform (ex officio
state board of pardons) (d)

---

[1] The W. Va. Legislature in 1925 enacted a law providing for a Crippled Children's Council. Composed of representatives of State Boards of Education, Health, Control and Children's Guardians, one each, and the three citizens appointed by Governor upon recommendation of Rotary or other social agencies. No money appropriated this year for organization.
C. L. STONAKER, *Executive Secretary.*

Child Labor Commission (d)
Commissioner of Child and Animal Protection
(semi-official)

VARIATIONS

Departments of education frequently control, supervise, or provide educational facilities for the deaf, dumb, blind, and physically handicapped.

Departments of health frequently supervise hospitals, and always have powers of inspection over sanitary features of state institutions, and even over the physical condition of inmates.

War veterans who are dependent are often independently provided for in soldiers' homes managed separately, and by veterans bureaus independent of other branches.

Child welfare is often a function of the health department, and especially so where the state has accepted the provisions of the Smith-Lever Act, and has placed its administration in the health department.

Other branches, such as the department of agriculture, will often be found related in some manner to public welfare activities.

CHAPTER V

TYPES OF STATE SYSTEMS

IN a general view of state systems many significant details which reside in particular systems
are hidden. The states selected for this chapter
are those which have, for the most part, well developed systems representative of the larger differences to be found in organization throughout
the country. They are not selected primarily because of remarkable achievements in the field of
public welfare, but many of them have made pio-
neer advances in organization, administration, and
extension of public welfare work. The most significant development in the field at the present
time is in the close relationship evolving between
state agencies and local instrumentalities of government. Even private agencies are coming into
the scheme in definite relationships. The matter
of local organization was not dealt with extensively in the preceding chapters. In this chapter
it is given such attention as a study of the rather
formal aspects of the work affords. Two state
departments omitted in this chapter, Pennsylvania
and North Carolina, are reserved for separate
chapters, carrying the detailed description a step
further for illustrative purposes. The following systems will serve to illustrate all types now
current.

KEY LEGENDS FOR CHARTS

Key to Symbols Used in Charts VIII to XVII.

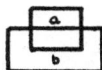

State Department
   a - Director or Chief
   b - Departmental Staff and Organization.

Professional Board.

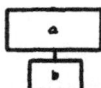

Lay Board.
   a - The Board
   b - Chief Executive Officer.

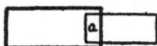

a - Indicates Common or Interlocking Membership.

Lesser Agencies, from the Standpoint of Public Welfare, (of Various Types)

Indicates Chiefly Supervisory Control, or Those Exclusively of Social Technique

Indicates Complete Control of an Institution by an Agency

Indicates Limited Control [Business or Financial Management]

Supervisory Powers Exercised by General State Officers, [Attorney General, Treasurer, etc.]

THE MASSACHUSETTS PLAN

ORGANIZATION AND PERSONNEL

a. Governor and Council

b. Supervisor of Administration

c. Departments of State, Treasurer, Attorney General, Civil Service, etc., having general supervision of specific activities

d. Probation Commission

e. Department of Health

f. Public Health Council

g. Department of Corrections

h. Parole and Pardon Board

i. Department of Public Welfare

j. Advisory Board of Public Welfare

k. Division of Aid and Relief

l. Board of Trustees of the State Infirmary within the Division of Aid and Relief

m. Division of Juvenile Training, and Trustees of the Massachusetts Training Schools

n. Division of Child Guardianship

o. Board of Trustees of the Massachusetts Hospital School within the Division of Child Guardianship

p. Department of Mental Diseases

q. Advisory Commission on Mental Diseases

NOTE—a, a, a, etc., Boards of Trustees of state institutions.
b, b, Indicates relationship of other departments to the ones illustrated.

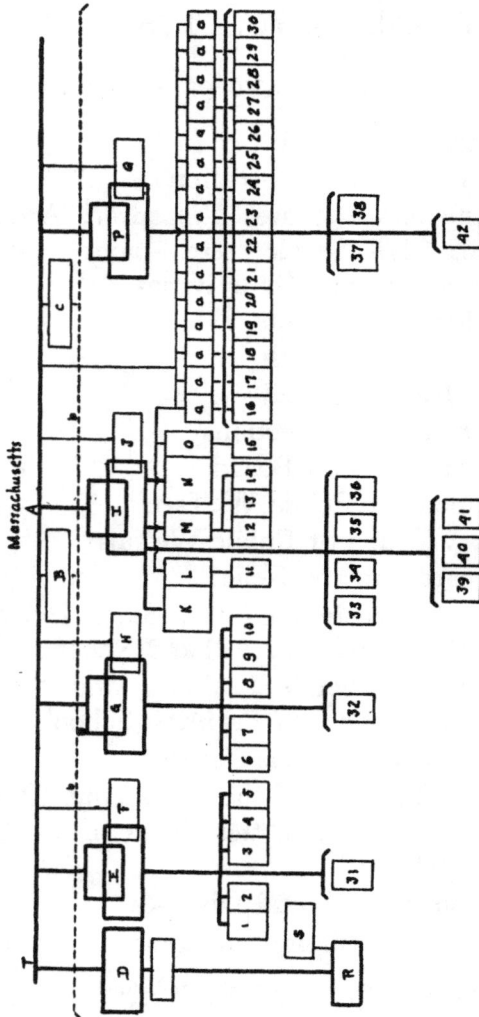

Massachusetts

Chart XIII

r. Local Probation Officers controlled by the Probation Commission

s. Local courts of the state

t. Supreme Court Justices

INSTITUTIONS

1. State Sanitarium at Rutland
2. State Sanitarium at North Reading
3. State Sanitarium at Lakeville
4. State Sanitarium at Westfield
5. Penkese Hospital
6. State Prison
7. Massachusetts Reformatory
8. Reformatory for Women
9. Prison Camp and Hospital
10. State Farm
11. State Infirmary
12. Lyman School for Boys
13. Industrial School for Boys
14. Industrial School for Girls
15. Massachusetts Hospital School
16. Boston Psychopathic Hospital
17. Boston State Hospital
18. Dawes State Hospital
19. Foxborough State Hospital
20. Gardner State Colony
21. Massachusetts School for the Feeble Minded
22. Medfield State Hospital
23. Manson State Hospital
24. Norfolk State Hospital

25. Northampton State Hospital
26. Tannton State Hospital
27. Westborough State Hospital
28. Worcester State Hospital
29. Wrentham State School
30. Grafton State Hospital
31. Local Tuberculosis Institutions
32. Local Prisons and Jails
33. County Training Schools
34. City and Town Outdoor Relief
35. City and Town Charitable Institutions
36. City and Town Housing and Town Planning Boards
37. Local Hospitals for Mental Defectives
38. Asylums and Places of Detention for Mental Defectives
39. Maternity Hospitals (private)
40. Child Caring Agencies (private)
41. Private Chartered Agencies
42. Private Hospitals for Mental Defectives

THE DEPARTMENT OF PUBLIC WELFARE[1]

DIVISIONS AND PERSONNEL

1. The Commissioner of Public Welfare
2. The Advisory Board of Public Welfare
3. The three divisions prescribed by law, and

[1] Annals, loc. cit. p. 119. Richard K. Connant, "The Massachusetts Department of Public Welfare."

such others as the Commissioner may organize from time to time

    a. Division of Aid and Relief, with subdi-
vision of Mothers' Aid and Social Service

    b. Division of Juvenile Training

    c. Division of Child Guardianship, with sub-
division of Investigation

    d. Additional subdivisions within the De-
partment include the work of Licensing,
and Housing and Town Planning

4. Five state institutions and their respective
governing boards

THE COMMISSIONER OF PUBLIC WELFARE

Appointed by the governor with the advice and
consent of the Council

Term of office, five years

Maximum salary $6,000

The Commissioner is executive head of the Department

He is head ex officio, of the Advisory Board of
Public Welfare

He may appoint officials, agents, clerks, and
other employees of the Department, except as
otherwise provided by law (subject to civil
service, and certain powers of the governor)
(Appointments to the Divisions of Aid and
Relief and Child Guardianship shall be made
in consultation with the directors of those
divisions.)

ADVISORY BOARD OF PUBLIC WELFARE

Six members, with the Commissioner, ex officio,
chairman and the seventh member. Two members must be women.

Appointed by the governor with the advice and
consent of the Council

Terms of office, three years

No salaries paid. Compensation allowed for
expenses in the discharge of duties

The Board shall assist the Commissioner in the
work of the Department, investigate questions
arising in connection therewith, and shall consider, formulate, and recommend such proposals
as may seem feasible for the further work of
the Department. It shall advise the Commissioner concerning the policies of the Department and shall make recommendations concerning the service or administration of any division
thereof. The Board shall meet at least once a
month and at such other time as it may determine by its rules, and when requested by the
Commissioner, or any three members. It shall
approve the rules and regulations governing the
conduct of the Department submitted by the
Commissioner. On approval of a majority of
the Board they shall become effective. It shall
hear and pass on objections to the rulings.
When so directed by the governor, it may assume and exercise powers and perform the

duties of the board of trustees of any institution under the supervision of or placed in the Department.

Many functions are allotted to the Department to be exercised "by the Commissioner and Board."

DIVISIONS OF THE DEPARTMENT

Aid and Relief

Director appointed, salary allotted, and tenure determined by the Commissioner, with the consent of the Governor and Council

Perform the duties required by law relative to the state adult poor, under supervision and direction of the Commissioner

Board of Trustees of State Infirmary

Appointed by the Governor with the advice and consent of the Council

Terms of office, three years

Unpaid, compensation allowed for expenses incurred in discharge of duties

Seven members, including five men and two women

Shall be a part of the Division of Aid and Relief

Division of Child Guardianship

Director appointed, salary allotted, and tenure fixed by the Commissioner with the advice and consent of the Governor and Council

Performs, the duties required by law relative to children under the supervision and control of the Commissioner

Board of Trustees of the Massachusetts Hospital School

Appointed by the governor, with the advice and consent of the council

Terms of office, five years

Unpaid, compensation allowed for expenses while discharging official duties

Number of members, five

Shall be supervised by, and be a part of, the Division of Child Guardianship

Division of Juvenile Training

Personnel of the division the same as the personnel of the Board of Directors of the Massachusetts Training Schools

Director designated by the governor from the board membership

Members appointed by the governor

Salaries and tenure the same as salaries and tenure while acting on the Board of Directors.

STATE INSTITUTIONS GOVERNED BY THE
DEPARTMENT

See numbers 11 to 15, inclusive, in the chart.

The "Advisory Board" in this department resembles a "lay board" in constitution, but lacks the power to select the chief executive of the department, and delegates no powers to him. In its advisory, legislative, and judicial capacities, however, it resembles other lay boards. Departments in Massachusetts were established in 1919. They differ considerably from departments like those in Illinois.

THE NEW YORK PLAN[2]

a. Governor and Senate
b. Supreme Court Justices
c. Prison Association of New York
d. Commission on New Prisons
e. Superintendent of State's Prisons
f. Parole Board
g. Prison Commission
h. Probation Commission
i. Department of Purchase
j. Commission for Mental Defectives
k. State Board of Charities
l. State Comptroller
m. Child Welfare Commission
n. Hospital Development Commission
o. Department of Education
p. Hospital Commission
q. State Charities Aid Association
r. Boards of County Supervisors
s. County (Juvenile) Court
t. County Superintendents of the Poor

[2] Annals, loc. cit., p. 113. Richard W. Wallace, "The New York State System and It's Problem of Reorganization."

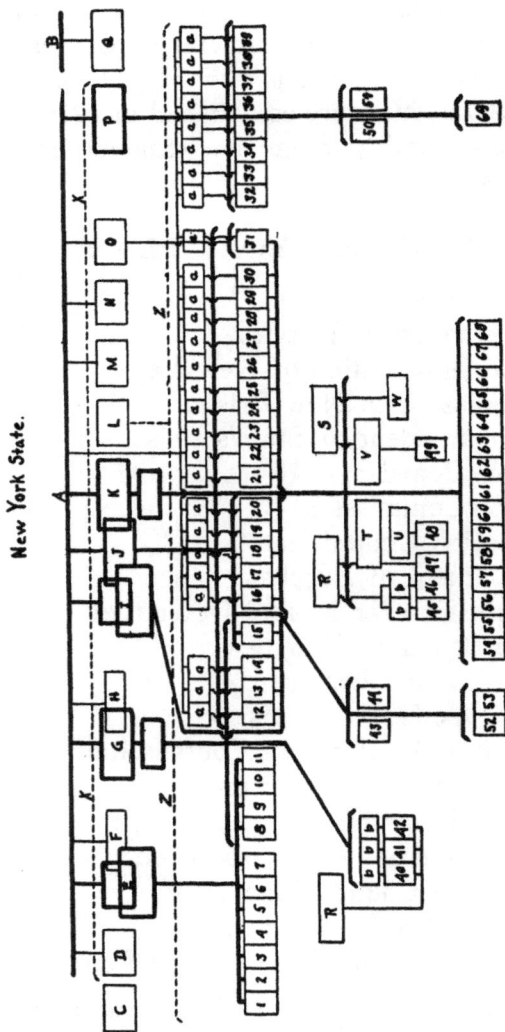

Chart XIII.

u. District Supervisors of the Poor

v. County Boards of Child Welfare

w. Probation Officers

x, x. Supervisory and other relations of State Treasurer, Attorney General, and other state officers to the general system

z, z. Supervisory relations of State Comptroller over finances of State Institutions.

INSTITUTIONS

1. Bureau of Identification
2. Dannemora State Hospital
3. Matteawan State Hospital
4. State Farm for Women
5. State Prison for Women (Auburn)
6. Wingate Prison
7. Prison for the Condemned
8. Auburn Prison
9. Clinton Prison
10. Sing Sing Prison
11. Great Meadows Prison
12. Western House of Refuge for Women (Albion)
13. New York State Reformatory for Women (Bedford Hills)
14. New York State Reformatory (Elmira)
15. Institution for Defective Delinquents (Napanoch)

NOTE—a, a, a, etc., Boards of managers for state institutions.
b, b, b, etc., Trustees, Sheriffs, and managers of local institutions.

16. State School for Mental Defectives (Syracuse)
17. State School for Mental Defectives (Newark)
18. State School for Mental Defectives (Rome)
19. Letchworth Village
20. State Farm Colony for Mental Defectives
21. State Agricultural and Industrial School (Industry)
22. New York State Training School for Girls (Hudson)
23. New York House of Refuge (Randall's Island)
24. New York State Soldiers' and Sailors' Home (Bath)
25. New York State Womens' Relief Corps Home (Oxford)
26. Thomas Indian School (Iroquois)
27. New York State Hospital for Crippled and Deformed Children (West Haverstraw)
28. New York State Hospital for the Treatment of Incipient Pulmonary Tuberculosis (Raybrook)
29. New York City Reformatory for Misdemeanants
30. Society for the Reformation of Juvenile Delinquents in the City of New York
31. New York State School for the Blind (Batavia)

32. State Hospital for the Poor and Indigent Insane
33. Mohansic State Hospital
34. Central Islip State Hospital
35. Kings Park State Hospital
36. Middleton State Homeopathic Hospital
37. Gowonda State Homeopathic Hospital
38. Brooklyn State Hospital
39. Manhattan State Hospital.

LOCAL INSTITUTIONS

40. County Jails
41. City Jails and Police Stations
42. Lockups
43. Coöperative Clinics, municipal and state
44. Local Institutions for Mental Defectives
45. County Tuberculosis Hospitals
46. Colonies for Inebriates, etc.
47. Almshouses
48. Outdoor Poor Relief
49. Mothers' Pensions and Child Welfare
50. Local Institutions for the Insane
51. Places of Detention of Insane.

PRIVATE INSTITUTIONS

52. Private Institutions for Mental Defectives licensed by the Commission
53. Coöperative Clinics in Incorporated Hospitals
54. Day Nurseries
55. Dispensaries

56. Fresh Air Charities
57. Homes for the Aged
58. Homes for Children
59. Homes and Schools for the Blind
60. Hospitals
61. Industrial Schools
62. Infant Asylums and Hospitals
63. Institutions for Mental Defectives and Epileptics
64. Placing Out and Boarding Out Agencies
65. Reformatories for Adults
66. Schools for the Deaf
67. Temporary and Special Homes for Children
68. Temporary Homes for Adults
69. Private Places of Detention for the Insane.

LOCAL ORGANIZATIONS

The State Board of Charities is in most extensive contact with local units of administration. The typical organization is illustrated in the chart. Variations in greater or less degree are the rule for particular cities or counties. In general, the County Superintendent of the Poor is the chief local poor official. He supervises county relief and acts as superintendent of the county poor asylum. The actual distribution of doles is in the hands of the district supervisors, who care for outside cases, and apply temporary or emergency relief. The County (Juvenile) Courts appoint child welfare boards, for the purpose of administering mothers' pensions, if pensions are provided by the county. The County Board of Supervisors is the ultimate authority in allocating funds for county institutions, and for poor relief. The various officials, particularly the County Superintendent of the Poor, may be elected by popular vote, or may be appointed by the Commissioners.

County jails are supervised by the Prison Commission, and occasionally other institutions by other agencies.

It is exceedingly difficult to chart all the details of the New York system. They differ from year to year, and many systematic attempts have been made to reorganize. Agencies not included in the chart are the following: State Board of Health, which has relations to state sanitaria similar to those of the Commissioner of Education to the schools for defectives; Salary Classification Commission; Building Improvement Commission; Board of Classification; New York State Commission for the Blind.

THE MINNESOTA PLAN

INSTITUTIONS

1. Home School for Girls
2. Reformatory for Women
3. State's Prison

NOTE—a, a, a, etc., Superintendents, or chief executive officers of institutions.
    b. Controlling boards of the normal schools of the state.
    c. Trustees for the Soldiers' Home
    d. Board of Capitol Commissioners.

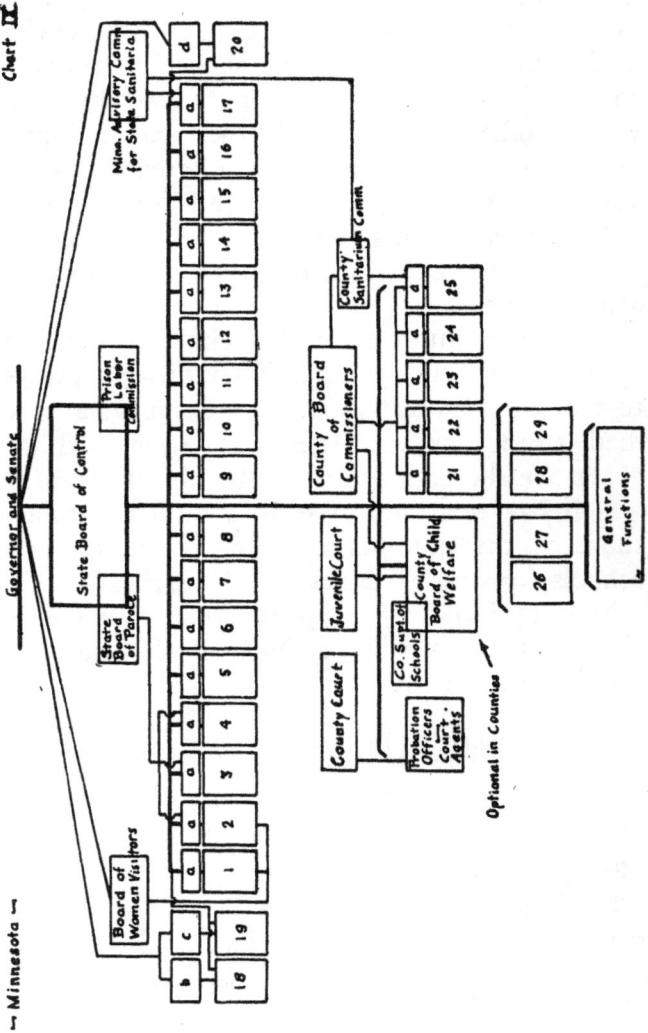

Chart II

~ Minnesota ~

 4. Reformatory
 5. State Training School
 6. State Public School
 7. State School for the Deaf
 8. State School for the Blind
 9. State Hospital for Crippled Children
10. Anoka Asylum
11. Hastings Asylum
12. Wilmar Asylum
13. School for the Feeble-Minded
14. Fergus Falls Hospital
15. Rochester Hospital
16. St. Peters Hospital
17. State Sanitarium
18. Normal schools of the state
19. Soldiers' Home
20. State Capitol Buildings.

LOCAL INSTITUTIONS
21. County jails
22. Lockups
23. Infirmaries
24. Hospitals
25. Asylums.

PRIVATE INSTITUTIONS
26. Maternity Hospitals
27. Infant Boarding Homes
28. Child Caring and Placing Agencies
29. Agencies transporting children into and out of the state.

LOCAL ORGANIZATIONS

County child welfare boards are established by the state board at the request of county commissioners. They consist of three appointees of the state board, a representative of the commissioners, and the county superintendent of schools. They administer mothers' pensions, probation and parole for the juvenile court, and act as agent for the Board of Control in the counties. Court agents act with the state board where no county board exists. The county commissioners govern local institutions. The county Sanitarium Commission administers county sanitaria where they exist.

THE BOARD OF CONTROL

The Board consists of five members, two of whom must be women. It was increased from three to five several years ago, and the legislation of 1923 provides that it shall be reduced to three again as soon as the terms of the next two retiring members expire.

Tenure, six years, and until successors qualify.

Salary, $4500 per year, and all expenses incurred in the discharge of official duties.

Appointed by the Governor with the consent of the Senate.

Vacancies filled as in the case of regular appointments.

Members removable by the Governor for malfeasance, no feasance, or for any cause rendering unfit to discharge official duties.

Bonds, approved by the Governor, required to the sum of $25,000.

Must devote whole time to office, and accept no other lucrative employment.

Member whose term is first to expire shall be chairman of the board.

Books and affairs of the board are subject to examination by the public examiner.

The board is to be provided with suitably furnished offices at the seat of government, and may procure all the supplies needed for its own activities.

It shall have an official seal, be a body corporate, sue and be sued, etc.

A large share of the functions enumerated in Appendix II are attributable to this board. The board resembles in its constitution and powers those of Wisconsin and Iowa.

THE KENTUCKY PLAN

STATE INSTITUTIONS

1. Eastern State Hospital
2. Central State Hospital
3. Western State Hospital
4. Feeble-Minded Institute
5. State School for Girls

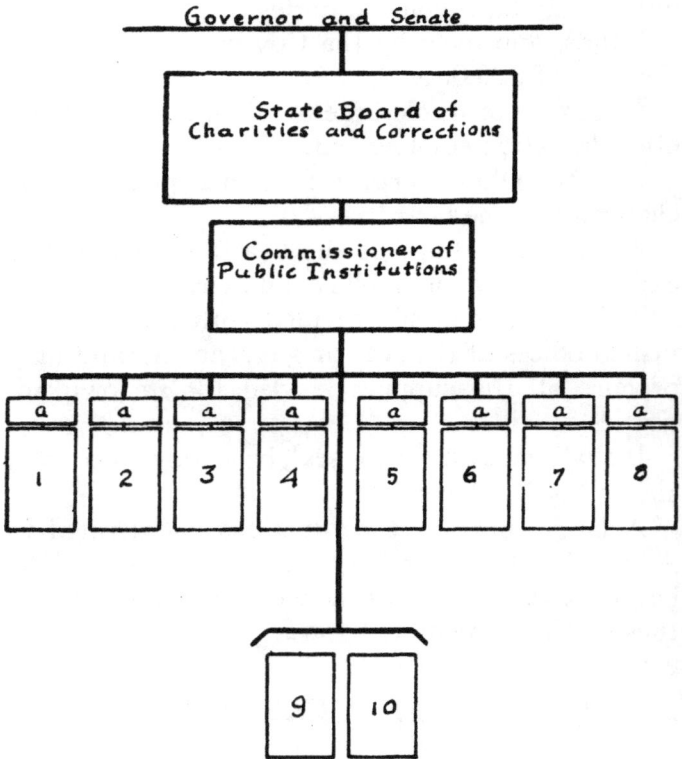

—• Kentucky •• •—

Chart X

6. State Reformatory
7. State Penitentiary.

PRIVATE INSTITUTIONS

8. All agencies soliciting funds within the state
9. All agencies supported in whole or in part from public funds.

THE STATE BOARD OF CHARITIES AND CORRECTIONS

Number of members eight, two of whom must be women, and not more than four from the same political party.

Appointed by the Governor with the consent of the Senate.

Tenure, four years.

Unsalaried, compensation allowed for expenses incurred in the discharge of official duties.

Vacancies filled by the Governor ad interim between Senate sessions; otherwise in manner of original appointments.

Members removable by the Governor for cause after public hearing.

All members must be residents of Kentucky, and not less than thirty years of age.

The Board is to be provided with a suite of offices at the Capitol Building.

Meet monthly, select own chairman annually, and record all proceedings.

Select a "Commissioner of Public Institutions" who is to be the Board's executive officer.

Appoint institutional superintendents, adopt rules and regulations for institutional management, but permit the superintendent a free hand in institutional affairs, holding him strictly accountable for all the details of management. Provide a non-partisan control of institutions.

License private organizations soliciting funds within the state.

Supervise all organizations supported from public funds.

The principles underlying the Kentucky organization are excellent. The system is relatively undeveloped, and the work is almost exclusively confined to management of state institutions. It is not related to local governmental agencies; and touches private agencies only in certain matters of financial supervision. A gradual extension of functions beyond institutional spheres would doubtless be a healthy sign of development in Kentucky. The plan seems excellently adapted to a state where the political situation is relatively unstable.

THE CALIFORNIA PLAN

STATE INSTITUTIONS

1. San Quentin State Prison
2. Folsom State Prison

3. Industrial Home for the Adult Blind
4. California School for Girls
5. Whittier State School
6. State Industrial Farm for Women
7. Preston School of Industry
8. Pacific Colony
9. Sonoma State School
10. Stockton State Hospital
11. Southern California State Hospital
12. Norwalk State Hospital
13. Napa State Hospital
14. Mendocino State Hospital
15. Agnews State Hospital.

LOCAL INSTITUTIONS

16. County Hospitals
17. County Jails
18. County Almshouses (Supervised by State Department)
19. City Prisons.

PRIVATE INSTITUTIONS

20. Institutions Receiving State Aid for the Care of Orphaned Children
21. Private Child Placing Agencies
22. Maternity Homes and Hospitals (Transferred to supervision of State Board of Health).

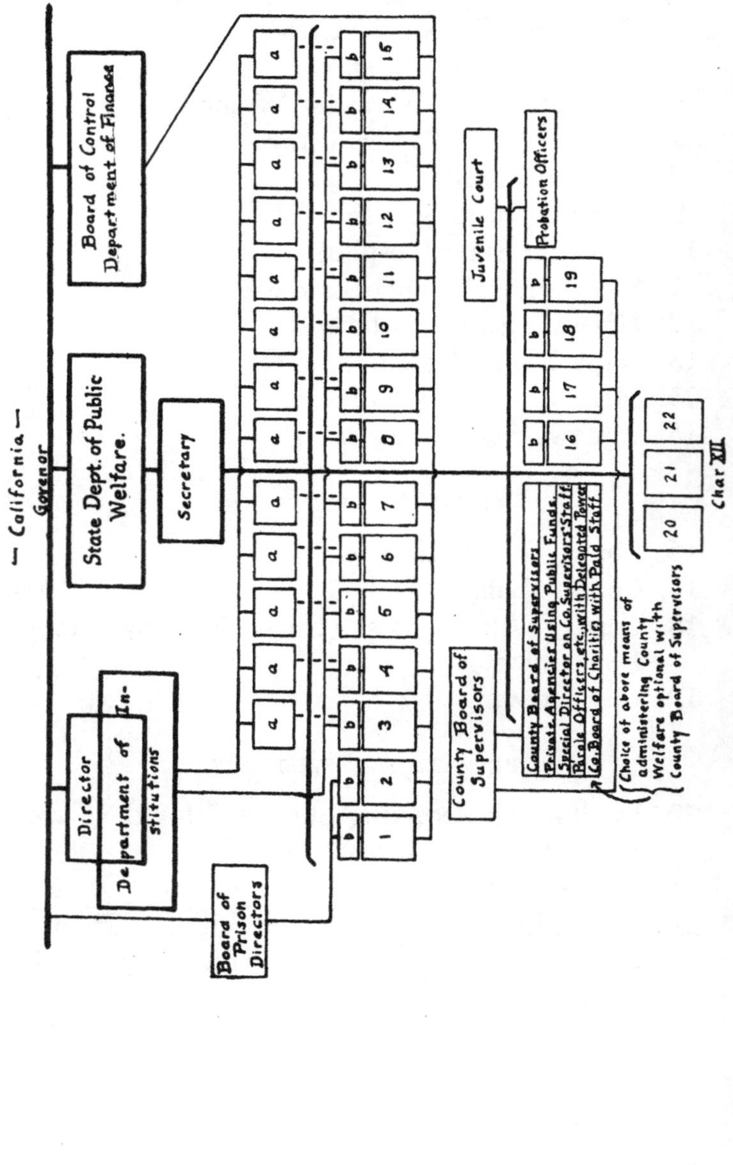

— California —
Governor

Board of Control
Department of Finance

State Dept. of Public
Welfare.

Secretary

Director
Department of In-
stitutions

Board of
Prison
Directors

Juvenile Court

Probation Officers

County Board of
Supervisors

County Board of Supervisors
Private Agencies using Public Funds
Special Director an Co-Supervisors Staff
Rural Officers, etc., with Delegated Power
Co. Board of Charities with Paid Staff

Choice of above means of
administering County
Welfare optional with
County Board of Supervisors

Chart XII

COUNTY ORGANIZATION

The State Department is stimulating better county organization. The five types which exist in order of their apparent value are: (1) County Board of Charity with its own paid and expert staff. (2) Director of Welfare. An official subject to the County Commissioners, and with status as executive on their staff. (3) Delegation of additional authority by the county commissioners to existing officials, such as school attendance officers, or court probation agents, so that they shall have wider powers to administer relief and do welfare work. (4) Allotment of funds to private agencies to be spent under public supervision. (5) Actual administration of funds by individual county commissioners, as has been done since the beginning. Obviously, progress toward the first plan is the desire of the state board. All authority rests with the county commissioners, and any agency authorized to administer public welfare would derive its powers from the board of commissioners.

THE NEW JERSEY PLAN

STATE DEPARTMENT OF INSTITUTIONS
AND AGENCIES

a. Governor and Senate
b. State Board of Control (unsalaried)

c. Commissioner, appointed by the Board of Control (salaried)

d, d, d, etc., Boards of Trustees for the several state institutions, all appointed by the Board of Control (unsalaried)

e. State Board of Children's Guardians, appointed by the Board of Control (unsalaried)

f. Secretary of the Board of Children's Guardians (salaried)

g. State and local relationships with officials and agencies dealing with children

h. Institutions of the state (total of nine)

(There is also a board similar to the Board of Children's Guardians called the Commission for the Amelioration of the Condition of the Blind).

THE MICHIGAN PLAN

STATE WELFARE DEPARTMENT

a. Governor and Senate

b. State Administrative Board (Governor, Secretary of State, State Treasurer, Auditor General, Attorney General, State Highway Commissioner, Superintendent of Public Instruction

c. Director of Public Welfare, appointed by the Governor and Senate

d. Welfare Department, consisting of the administrative staff, and the several commissions *e.* State Hospital Commission

f. State Prison Commission

g. State Corrections Commission

h. State Institutions Commission

i. State Welfare Commission

j. Deputy Director of Welfare, and Secretary of the State Welfare Commission

k. County agents, and relationships with local courts and institutions

l. Superintendents of State Institutions, appointed by the Governor on recommendation of the Commissions supervising

m. Institutions of the state, seventeen in all.

Members of all the state commissions are chosen by the Governor and Senate, as are institutional heads. Their work and the work of the director of welfare and his deputy are subject to constant supervision and check by the State Administrative Board. Solely from the standpoint of organization, this seems to place the welfare department in the hands of the Governor and his Administrative Board, reducing the functions of the Department as such to those of collecting statistics and making reports. The Commissions have judicial and supervisory functions, but purchasing, control of personnel, and appointments of institutional executives are not functions of the commissions or the department, except in an advisory way.

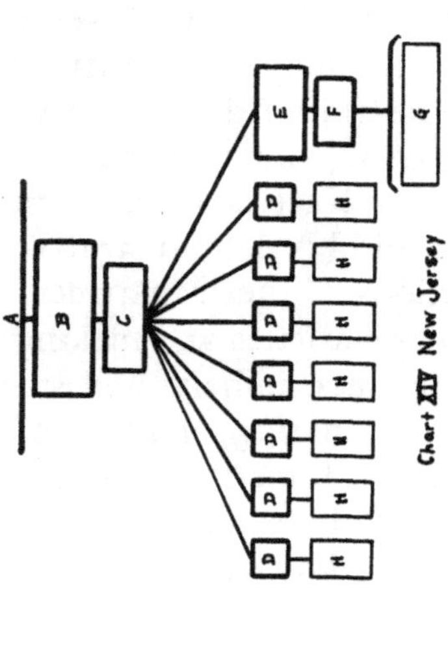

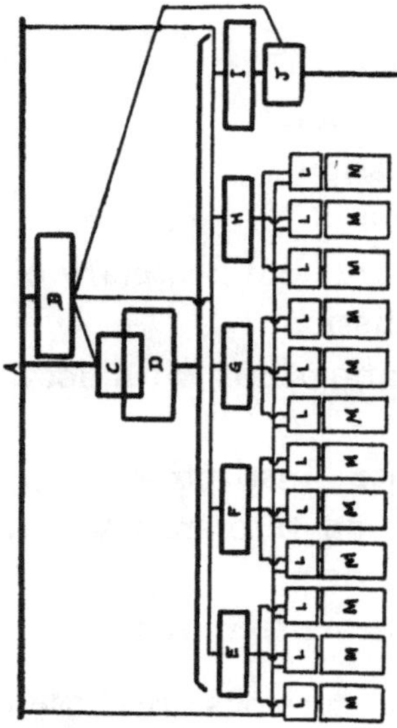

Chart XV Michigan.

Chart XIII Mississippi.

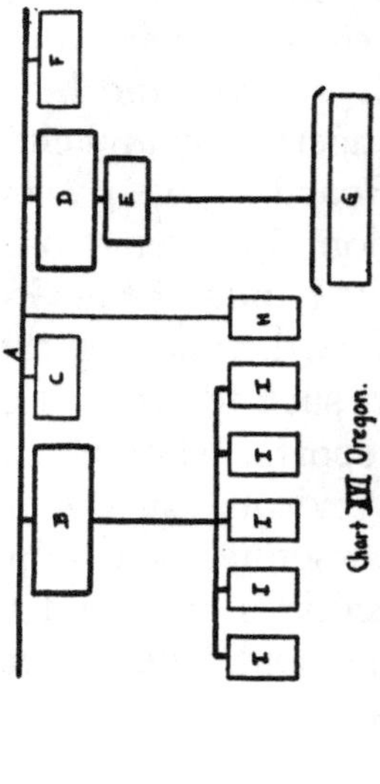

Chart XIV New Jersey

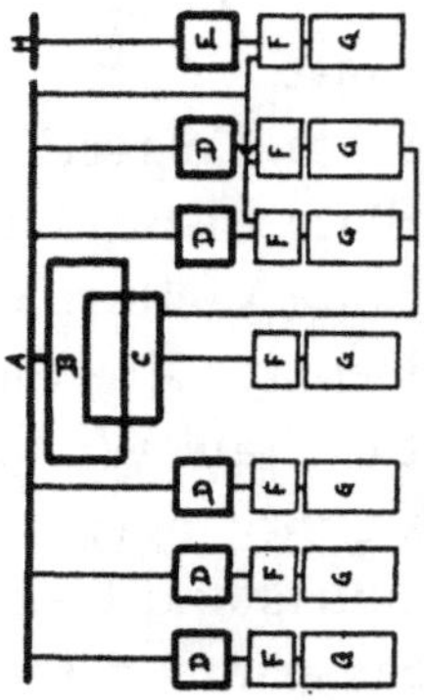

Chart XII Oregon.

THE OREGON PLAN

a. Governor
b. Board of Control (Governor, Secretary of State, Attorney General)
c. Board of Parole
d. Child Welfare Commission (unsalaried)
e. Secretary of the Child Welfare Commission (salaried)
f. Child Labor Commission
g. Local relationships of the Child Welfare Commission with courts and agencies for child care.
h. State Prison, under control of the Governor
i. Other state institutions

In Oregon the two dominant phases of welfare work are organized separately, that relating to institutional control, and that relating to community and local work. The next step will be to unite these in some acceptable manner.

THE MISSISSIPPI PLAN

a. Governor
b. State Board of Health (twelve physicians appointed by the Governor) (unsalaried)
c. "Executive Committee" (three physicians comprising a committee of the board to carry on the functions of the board between meetings)

d. Boards of Trustees (appointed by the Governor)

e. Trustees of the State Prison (elected by the people)

f. Superintendents of state institutions (those of three institutions are selected by the Governor; the others by the governing boards)

g. State Institutions

h. People of the State

The State Board of Health is also an advisory board to the two "charity" hospitals. This illustrates the total absence of any genuine central administrative or supervisory body for public welfare, except as the Governor effects unified administration.

CHAPTER VI

FUNCTIONS OF PUBLIC WELFARE AGENCIES

THE most direct method of understanding the reach and the power of the thing we call public welfare is undoubtedly through a study of the functions which present agencies exercise. Many who read this chapter will be surprised by the scope and potential power of this relatively new state service,—new in many of its connotations, at any rate. Obviously, this chapter does not present a typical picture of the situation in any single state in the Union. It is a composite picture, within which nearly every state will find its limits somewhere. There may be some items not included even in this comprehensive list. If so, they are probably not greatly different in kind from some that are listed. Functions could not be here stated in legal terminology exclusively. If that were attempted throughout, the differences in phraseology employed everywhere would make tedious duplication of items unavoidable. Items were classified together whenever legal terminology connoted common intent; and then described, as here given, in appropriate general terms. This method of course prevents giving recognition to the prevalence of any particular kind of statutory provision.

The classification here attempted is three-fold in nature. Functions are grouped according to whether they apply to *institutions and agencies*— the instrumentalities of welfare, *objects of welfare* —individuals, groups, classes, wards, communities, or are *otherwise characterized.*

INSTITUTIONS

Institutions which are the objects of public welfare are three-fold in kind: *state institutions, local institutions,* and *private institutions.*

STATE INSTITUTIONS

Prisons (many types)
Prison farms, camps, colonies, factories
Reformatories and training schools
Detention homes (several types)
State schools and receiving homes
Hospitals for crippled, deformed and defective
Hospitals for sick and injured
Hospitals for special diseases (tuberculosis, leprosy, etc.)
Camps, colonies, farms for tuberculous and other sick
Schools for the deaf, dumb, blind, and physically handicapped
Hospitals for the insane, epileptic, and mentally defective
Asylums for the insane, epileptic, and mentally defective

Colonies and farms for the insane, epileptic, and mentally defective
Clinics and dispensaries for all purposes
Research and service laboratories.

STATE AGENCIES

Boards of managers and all officials connected with institutions
Many special boards, officers, and other agencies associated with field work, supervision, etc.

LOCAL INSTITUTIONS

Jails, prisons, pens, lockups, etc.
Prison camps, road crews, shops, quarries, etc.
Almshouses, infirmaries, asylums, poor farms, etc.
Reformatories and workhouses
Detention homes and places
Hospitals for the insane and epileptic
Asylums, camps, colonies, for the insane, epileptic, and feeble minded
Schools, farms, colonies, for the physically handicapped and feeble-minded
Hospitals for the sick and injured
Clinics, dispensaries, laboratories.

LOCAL AGENCIES

Boards of county supervisors and commissioners
Institutional trustees and officers
Superintendents and overseers of the poor
Probation and attendance officers

Boards of child welfare, charities and corrections, or public welfare for cities and counties

Agents, representatives, and employees of these boards

Agents, representatives, and officials of local courts

County and juvenile courts

Superintendents of public welfare

Township trustees, etc.

PRIVATE INSTITUTIONS

Day nurseries

Dispensaries

Fresh air charities

Permanent and temporary homes for the aged

Permanent, temporary, and special homes for children

Homes and schools for the blind

Hospitals for the sick and insane

Industrial schools for juvenile and adult offenders

Infant asylums and hospitals

Maternity homes and hospitals

Institutions for mental defectives and epileptics

Placing-out and boarding-out agencies for children

Reformatories for adults

Schools for the deaf

Homes for adults, temporary and permanent

Agencies receiving state aid

Chartered, incorporated, licensed agencies

Agencies soliciting public funds
Other private welfare agencies of all kinds.

PRIVATE OFFICIALS AND AGENCIES

Societies and corporations, with their managing boards, officials, or any others responsible for the foregoing institutions.

POWERS AND DUTIES

STATE INSTITUTIONS

1. Maintain and govern specified state institutions
2. Supervise and direct the management of them
3. Have care and custody of all property of the state related to them
4. Formulate the objects for which institutions are established and make rules and regulations for the management of institutions in accordance with the objects; including business, financial, and social phases of management
5. Visit and inspect institutions regularly (monthly, quarterly, annually, etc.) to determine: (a) Whether employees are competent and faithful. (b) Inmates are properly cared for and governed. (c) Whether accounts, books, and vouchers are properly kept. (d) Whether business affairs are properly conducted
6. Establish and maintain a system, and pre-

scribe forms for the keeping of books, records, accounts, and for the rendering of all reports

7. Annually cause all accounts to be examined by an expert accountant. Annually inventory and appraise all property, and classify as to kinds, amount, and value

8. Hold any property in trust for the benefit of inmates of institutions, or for the benefit of institutions, and dispose of same in accordance with the terms of the trust

9. Appoint a secretary of the board (or dept.) to act as keeper of books and accounts, and advisor regarding physical properties; appoint necessary agents to visit, inspect, and report on institutions; appoint executive officers of institutions, including superintendents, wardens, stewards, purchasing agents, etc.; fix salaries of above appointees, determine qualifications, tenure, bonds, and prescribe duties, etc., except as otherwise prescribed by law

10. Fix the number and compensation of other employees; approve appointments by institutional heads; remove for cause; classify the service, and apply the classification uniformly to all institutions

11. Investigate complaints against institutional officers and management; have the power of compulsory processes in collecting evidence, etc.

12. Receive regular reports from institutional officers as prescribed by the board (or dept.)

13. Have full access to officers, employees, inmates, all departments, records, property, or places, with power to collect evidence from inmates, employees, records, or other sources

14. Examine plans and specifications for new buildings; aid in establishing new institutions; build and equip institutions; acquire and dispose of land and property according to law

15. Constitute (with the governor) a special board for districting the state according to the number of hospitals, asylums, or other types of institution within the state

16. Establish such education and moral training in correctional and custodial institutions as is for the best interests of the inmates

17. Establish and maintain courses of instruction at the school for the feeble-minded and epileptic children, and also for persons interested in the care and training of mentally retarded or defective children. Make rules and regulations for the conduct of courses

18. Establish training and instruction for the deaf, dumb, blind, and physically handicapped, in institutions and places throughout the state. Establish training and education in the state public school, and receiving home for children

19. Establish, maintain, and carry on prison in-

dustries to supply any needs of the state. Provide machinery, sell products, maintain and control a manufacturing revolving fund, prescribe methods of reimbursing prisoners for labor, supervise and regulate the employment of prisoners, and make full reports about operations, receipts, and expenditures.

20. Provide a merit system in prisons and reformatories to serve as the basis for discharges, pardons, and paroles

21. Assess the costs of maintaining certain classes of inmates in institutions, either to inmates or relatives, or to the counties of residence

22. Receive reports of special bodies investigating institutions, (such as Board of Women Visitors, Minnesota)

23. Arrange regular meetings of the officers of state institutions to discuss common problems, arrange common purchases, etc.

24. Make rules and regulations for the non-partisan administration of institutions

25. Ask for, and receive, the coöperation of other state departments in managing institutions

26. Permit and provide spiritual advice for inmates of institutions by advisors of inmates' own spiritual faith.

LOCAL INSTITUTIONS

1. Investigate and supervise all charitable, curative, reformatory, and penal institutions in

the counties and municipalities; and all industrial schools, hospitals, asylums, organized, existing, or to be organized

2. Visit and inspect all the preceding institutions and ascertain facts relative to population, care, cost, adequacy, sanitation, classification, treatment, reformation, causes of pauperism, insanity, and crime, and any data relative to particular institutions. Also ascertain facts relative to methods of treatment, government, official conduct of officers and directors, conditions of buildings and property, and other matters relative to usefulness and management

3. Make special investigations and reports, and inform the district attorney and Governor of any violation of law

4. Advise, suggest, and approve plans for county institutions; set standards and make regulations for all institutions regarding construction, repair, maintenance, safety, sanitation, fitness, etc.; approve establishment, purchase of site, and erection of buildings; inspect before occupancy, and regularly thereafter

5. Formulate rules for the government of institutions and the care of inmates; prescribe systems of record and report

6. Make recommendations to officers in charge of institutions relative to insufficiencies, necessary modifications, policy of administration,

etc. Order changes, and have the power to enforce compliance through the suspension of state allowances to the institution, and by legal processes. Approve local institutions before they become eligible for state aid

7. Regulate systems of account for business and financial transactions, statistics of institutions, and all matters of record. Require regular reports from officers and managers as deemed desirable, including reports from sheriffs and others responsible for the management of places of detention and punishment

8. Designate district jails for the use of larger units than the single county

9. Have free access to inmates, employees, records, and premises in carrying out functions of visitation, inspection, and supervision

10. Supervise official outdoor relief and the administration of mothers' pensions. Prescribe forms of record and report for the use of county boards of supervisors, their employees and agents, and other officials administering funds. Receive regular reports regarding persons cared for, kinds and amounts of relief, contracts made for support; approve or disapprove particular items in the administration of relief, approve allotments of state funds for relief; visit recipients of aid whether adults, children, aged, poor, mothers,

or others; supervise their treatment; advise and coöperate with courts and all local officials and agents administering aid or pensions concerning methods of investigation, oversight, bookkeeping, etc.

11. Receive reports from juvenile and other court probation officers respecting all cases on probation

12. Receive reports from appointing authorities regarding appointments made of institutional superintendents, or of county superintendents or county boards of public welfare, probation officers, etc.   Approve or disapprove appointments

13. Appoint local committees of visitors to inspect county institutions; to encourage and aid the local authorities in maintaining such institutions in an efficient manner; represent and aid the state board; report to it regularly; etc.

14. Recommend to local appointing authorities eligible candidates for superintendent of public welfare, boards of child welfare, charities, public welfare, etc., and approve appointments to these positions

15. Appoint local superintendents or boards of public (or child) welfare at the request of local boards of supervisors, or others; direct them in their work, prescribe duties, and remove for cause

16. Make rules and regulations for the appointments of probation officers and other local officials

17. Encourage county officials to establish county boards, provide for county superintendents of welfare, etc.

18. Coöperate with every local agency or official concerned with welfare administration; supervise in the performance of their functions, and with respect to methods of investigation, record keeping, and reports

19. Coöperate in training county superintendents of public welfare for their peculiar functions

20. Petition the courts for the removal of overseers of the poor, or members of county boards of supervisors who shall unreasonably neglect to comply with the provisions of the law

21. Meet regularly with county superintendents and officials to advise and consult with them with respect to the duties and problems of their office

22. Develop living quarters for citizens in accordance with the Homestead Law (Massachusetts)

23. Have general supervision over the work of the several city and town planning boards. (Massachusetts)

PRIVATE INSTITUTIONS

1. Investigate all petitions for charters or articles of incorporation by all charitable, eleemosynary, reformatory, custodial, curative institutions or agencies, and of corporations or associations desiring permission to care for dependent, delinquent, or neglected children. Approve or disapprove applications, and report to the authorities having power to grant same

2. Approve bonds, and prescribe rules and regulations for associations desiring to bring dependents (especially children) into the state, or remove them therefrom

3. Annually license, supervise, regulate, and inspect persons, associations or institutions receiving children for care, custody, training, or placement in private homes; agencies and institutions caring for mental defectives, insane, epileptic; agencies or institutions operated as infant boarding houses, maternity homes or hospitals; institutions for the aged, decrepit, and dependent; dispensaries; etc.

4. Annually license all institutions soliciting funds within the state. Investigate and report regarding agencies desiring to borrow money from the public for improvements. Prescribe forms for the filing of statements regarding solicitations of funds and property

for charitable and patriotic purposes, and issue certificates of registration

5. Send list of approved agencies for custody of children and others to county judges, and other officials concerned with commitments of dependents

6. Investigate and report with respect to all agencies supported in whole or in part from public funds; or agencies requesting state aid. On investigation ascertain:

   a. Whether all parts of the state are equally benefitted by institutions requiring state aid

   b. The merits of any and all requests for aid beyond the usual maintenance expenses

   c. Sources of public money received for the benefit of such institutions; manner of expenditure, and conditions of management

   d. Whether the objects of the institutions are being accomplished

   e. Whether the laws, and the rules and regulations of the state board are being obeyed

   f. Methods of industrial, educational, or moral training, and the adaptation of same to the needs of inmates

   g. Methods of government and discipline of inmates

   h. Qualifications and general conduct of officers and employees *i.* Any other matters regarding usefulness and management

7. Visit and inspect all private institutions enumerated, also including wayfarers lodges and public lodging houses. Demand all reports and information deemed desirable, and prescribe uniform methods of record and report for all purposes

8. Call attention of managers and trustees to any institutional abuses; and advise and compel correction

9. Visit, supervise, and control removals of wards in institutions, or those placed in family homes (particularly children, mothers, and mental defectives, when wards of private institutions and agencies).

MISCELLANEOUS TYPES

1. Supervise all state, county, municipal, or private institutions or associations that are charitable, eleemosynary, correctional, reformatory, curative; created for the care, custody, protection, or training of homeless, dependent, defective, delinquent, children or adults. Investigate and supervise the whole system of welfare, public or private, in the state

2. Make special investigations. Compel the production of evidence by compulsory processes.

Report findings and recommendations to the governor, institutional managers, or to the public

3. Prescribe uniform systems of record and registration, to secure accuracy, uniformity, and completeness of records. Collect records and statistics from institutions

4. Establish rules for the reception and retention of inmates in institutions. Receive reports regarding transfers, deaths, inquests, removals. Control custody and release of inmates

5. Approve expenditures of funds by institutions for special purposes

6. Approve plans for the erection of institutions receiving state support. Fix bonds in behalf of the state for contractors working on public buildings for the state, or any subdivision of it

7. Conduct conferences designed to effect co-ordination of officials and agencies in social work

8. Bring to the attention of officers and managers of institutions, standards and methods which may be helpful in government and administration, and beneficial to wards

9. By order, direct officers of institutions to correct objectionable features in the manner and within the time prescribed by the Commissioner (or Secretary). On failure to comply, take legal steps to effect a remedy

10. Establish and conduct mental clinics in connection with local agencies, private hospitals of an approved character, and state institutions

11. Allot sums due the counties, cities, or private agencies for the support of dependents chargeable to the state.

OBJECTS OF PUBLIC WELFARE

The second group consists of persons, classes of dependents, and social units about which social work is organized (not specifically related to persons in institutions, or to particular agencies).

CHILDREN AND MOTHERS

1. Administer, or supervise the administration of all laws designed for the protection of children. Promote and enforce laws for the protection of illegitimate, defective, dependent, neglected, and delinquent children. Safeguard the interests of children born, or about to be born, out of wedlock, and take legal steps to establish paternity. Coöperate to these ends with the juvenile court, all reputable child helping and placing agencies of a public and private nature, and take the initiative in matters involving the welfare of children whenever necessary

2. Administer or supervise the administration of all laws providing a system of mothers'

pensions in the state; allot pensions for the purpose of keeping children in the home

3. Place children in homes, hospitals, or special institutions for care, treatment, or training as is necessary for the good of the children

4. Receive notices of adoptions. Investigate and act for the good of the child if necessary. Consent to adoptions where no legal guardian exists

5. Receive the custody of and act as legal guardian over all children committed by the courts. Receive the custody of illegitimate and indigent children on petition of mother if deemed advisable. Control admissions to, and receive the custody of, all children committed to the state public school, or receiving home. Return unplaceable children to the courts committing them, or enter into arrangements with the courts for care in institutions or private boarding homes. Refuse guardianship when a better means of disposal is known

6. Place children in family homes. Visit, supervise, and order changes for children so placed by any agency, public or private in the state

7. Transfer children committed to homes or institutions as the welfare of the children demands

8. Receive reports from probation officers about all children committed by the courts

9. Receive notices and reports from all authorities, public and private, regarding all children placed in family homes, or any institutions for care or custody; and receive periodical reports of the result of supervision of such cases

10. Receive reports from physicians, undertakers, or public officials regarding cruel or inhuman treatment of children. Receive and investigate petitions of dependency, delinquency, etc., about children

11. Participate in the administration of the compulsory school attendance laws

12. Supervise and direct the child in employment

13. Provide institutional custody and treatment for juvenile offenders committed by the courts to state institutions for juvenile training; and the care of those children when on parole

14. Coöperate with the state board of health in administering the Smith-Lever act within the state

15. Appoint placement agents and other officials to administer the laws relative to children.

MENTAL DEFECTIVES, FEEBLE-MINDED AND INSANE

1. Make mental examinations and social investigations of all applicants for admission to state institutions, particularly institutions for the feeble-minded. Serve other institutions similarly on request, especially foster homes, or-

phanages, and public schools. Test and examine the mental and physical conditions of any state dependent

2. Administer the laws relative to the care, training, and treatment of mental defectives. Administer the state sterilization law

3. Accept the custody of all mental defectives committed by the courts, particularly children who are mentally defective, delinquent, neglected, and unsuitable for probation. Establish receiving homes for them, and arrange with private agencies for temporary care

4. Give instructions to patients in occupational therapy as deemed desirable

5. Coöperate with other state departments in providing education and training for the feeble-minded

6. Consent to the retention of feeble-minded and minors in almshouses under certain conditions

7. Establish a scheme of after care for the insane in coöperation with local authorities, and receive advance information from hospitals regarding discharges of the insane patients. Supervise all paroled persons from state hospitals and asylums for the insane, feeble-minded, and epileptic

8. Transfer the chronic indigent insane from state hospitals to county institutions, colonies, farms and private boarding houses. Author-

ize discharges of insane who are to be discharged as not cured

9. Order and compel the discharge of any person of unsound mind detained other than by court commitment.

POOR, AGED, AND INFIRM

1. Investigate and recommend suitability of free tuition and scholarships to individuals in state institutions of learning
2. Endeavor to cause all persons indigent and in need of available charities of the state to be cared for in the best manner possible
3. Supervise the aged, decrepit, and feebleminded seeking admission to any homes, retreats, or asylums. Investigate the condition of the poor seeking public aid, and devise measures for their relief
4. Send paupers within and without the state where they belong. Administer the laws with respect to the state and the alien poor, and the care of Indian poor persons
5. Direct public relief to unsettled persons in cities and towns.

THE PHYSICALLY HANDICAPPED

1. Appropriate funds for the attendance of blind children at schools and universities. Regulate the compulsory attendance of deaf and dumb between the ages of eight and twenty years at

the state school for deaf and blind. Recommend the disposition of available funds for the care of indigent cripple, tuberculous, blind, deaf, and dumb children and adults

2. Approve state support for indigent tuberculous patients.

3. Prepare a register of the blind; act as a board of industrial aid to visit the blind in their homes; contribute to their support; provide employment and education

4. Appoint field agents for the care of the blind.

PRISONERS, PAROLE, AND PROBATION

1. Examine and sign punishment records for state prisons

2. Control all paroles from state institutions, and all discharges from state industrial schools

3. Formulate rules for recording the conduct of prisoners. Act on applications for pardons and paroles. Consider cases of prisoners who have served the minimum sentence

4. Receive reports concerning persons on parole or probation from state parole or probation officers or agencies, or local officers or agencies who supervise paroled persons and persons on probation

5. Appoint field officers to supervise persons on parole or probation in the state.

TRANSFERS OF PERSONS IN CUSTODY

1. Supervise the transfers of prisoners in custody
2. Investigate and be heard before any order is made causing the transfer of any person in custody to any place
3. Direct the removal of any deaf or dumb person; any insane, epileptic, or feeble-minded person; any child, or other person in almshouses, or otherwise not in proper custody, to institutions suitable for their training, treatment, or care.

FINANCES RELATED TO PERSONS

1. Investigate the legal settlements of persons who may be state charges, but who have been supported, relieved, or buried by towns or cities
2. Determine pauper settlement when the question arises between counties. Decide all legal settlements, subject to appeal
3. Investigate the ability of inmates in asylums and hospitals to pay for their support, or be paid for by relatives and guardians. Assess costs against those able to pay, and use compulsory processes in making collections
4. Apportion charges for the support of inmates to counties of residence if inmates are not able to pay.

GUARDIANSHIP, AND MISCELLANEOUS ITEMS

1. Receive the guardianship of any persons committed to state institutions by the Federal courts, and look after same when on probation or parole
2. Receive the guardianship of prostitutes committed by the courts, and place in institutions or on probation
3. Authorize surgical operations where necessary and proper for the inmates of institutions. Function as guardians of inmates for such purposes.

RELATING TO COMMUNITIES

1. Organize the recreational facilities of rural communities, and promote wholesome recreation
2. Supervise commercial amusements in towns and counties
3. Coöperate with local, individual, and civic organizations and groups for child welfare, community betterment, education, and the organization of volunteer services

Functions not otherwise included in the preceding classifications are also important:

ORGANIZATION

1. Organize the board or department, establish bureaus, apportion duties within the provisions of the law

2. Particularly, establish a children's bureau for the better supervision and administration of child welfare laws

3. Select a trained investigator of social service problems to be known as the Commissioner of Public Welfare. (North Carolina)

4. Secure state agents, and other employees as needed; fix tenures, salaries, qualifications, duties, etc.

5. Cause to be printed rules and regulations for own procedure

6. Coöperate with other departments at necessary points. Employ an attorney for law enforcement, or call on the state or local prosecutors.

SUPERVISION

1. In general, supervise and coördinate the whole system of welfare administration, public and private, within the state.

STATISTICS

1. Collect, compile, analyse and publish, statistics relating to institutions and agencies; to dependent, delinquent, and defective classes, in and out of institutions; to insanity and crime, idiocy, feeble-mindedness, and other mental and physical defects for the purposes of recommending appropriate social legislation,

giving needed publicity about them and providing means for their amelioration and the protection of society.

OTHER INVESTIGATIONS

1. Consider and study the entire field of public welfare; advise executive officers of departments and institutions, and make recommendations to the general assembly
2. Study the problems of non-employment, poverty, vagrancy, housing conditions, crime, public amusements, care and treatment of prisoners, divorce and wife desertion, the social evil, and kindred subjects; their causes, treatment, prevention, and the prevention of hurtful social conditions generally
3. So far as possible, on the basis of such investigations, suggest and put into effect such remedial measures as may be of benefit to the Commonwealth in the prevention and ultimate eradication of anti-social acts and conditions
4. Gather, compile, and disseminate information embodying the best experience of penal, reformatory, and charitable institutions in this and other countries, and the best and most effective methods of caring for the insane and other defective classes
5. Provide for and encourage scientific investigations of the treatment of insanity, epilepsy,

and mental disorders by the staffs of institutions, and provide for statistical returns from institutions.

LEGISLATION AND REPORTS

1. Report to the governor at stated intervals, including all statistics of institutions, budget estimates, and reports of institutional officers. Include such other information as may be required, or pertinent to new legislation
2. Make recommendations to the governor and legislature regarding social legislation and the creation of new institutions.

LAW ENFORCEMENT AND GENERAL ADMINISTRATION

1. Administer any system of reparation provided for the relief of conditions caused by mine caves, floods, fire, or other casualty and consisting in a menace to public welfare and to society
2. Administer systems of legislation relating to all classes of wards, or types of institution and agency
3. Correlate state and county administration from the standpoint of uniformity, efficiency, related responsibilities, finances, etc. Allot state payments to the local governments for the support of wards chargeable to the state.

PUBLICITY AND EDUCATION

1. Issue bulletins, and in other ways inform the public about social conditions, and the proper treatment and remedy for social ills
2. Attend, either through members or agents, social service and similar conventions to assist in promoting helpful publicity tending to improve social conditions in the state.

CHAPTER VII

ATTAINABLE STANDARDS FOR STATE DEPARTMENTS

FROM a careful study of the previous chapters it is very clear that there is need for more uniform standards of organization and administration for state departments of public welfare in the United States. The purpose of such uniform standards will be to promote the effectiveness and comprehensiveness of public welfare services and economy of administration rather than to seek centralization and control. Uniform standards of the proper sort will, in the very nature of the case, permit of all needed and appropriate adaptation to local conditions. The purpose of this chapter is to emphasize the need for uniform standards; to discuss certain tendencies toward uniformity and to urge further study of the whole problem of organization and administration of public welfare in the United States.

Among the general conclusions that seem warranted are the following:

1. There is everywhere agreement that the problems of public welfare demand increasingly such organization and administrative plans as "the claims of humanity and the public good may require."

2. The great majority of the states, in recogni-

tion of this fact, have undertaken to work out their problems through some more definite and improved form of supervision and control.

3. But the outstanding feature in the whole field is perhaps the wide variation and almost complete lack of uniform methods, organization and scope of work undertaken.

4. In spite of wide variations there can be shown clearly certain common needs, purposes and prospects, manifestly susceptible to uniform treatment.

5. There are certain difficulties, both in present application and in historical development, that are common to all state departments.

6. The financial problem involved constitutes an increasingly important one in that it will include the expenditure of from one-sixth to one-fourth of state appropriations, exclusive of local, town and county funds and of many border-line charges.

7. A separate study will be necessary for the better understanding and organization of the financial administration and methods of institutions and state departments involved.

8. From all these conclusions it would seem wise to attempt some general statement as to the form and scope of the desired type of department to which the majority of states may conform.

9. There is urgent need for further study; for agreement on general purposes and plans and for

the recognition of the hard and difficult situations which may not seem to conform to theoretical discussions and ideals.

10. There are some indications that progress is not so rapid as it should be—because of economy, too much technique, and lack of education on the subject.

Concerning the general agreement that all states must go forward in the development of a program of public welfare, there is need for little discussion. There is no state which refuses to undertake something for its socially deficient in the unequal places of life. It would seem clear that any progressive state would prefer to undertake all efforts in the best possible way to obtain results and to conserve the energies and moneys of its citizens. It would seem, furthermore, that any progressive state would elect to work out such measures and methods as would not only serve its unfortunates, but prevent, or constantly reduce to its lowest possible limit, the socially deficient among its constituency, and thus render a twofold service to all its people. The constructive and preventive measures, therefore, take on the more important aspects, both from the view of democratic service and from the viewpoint of economy of funds. It is clear, furthermore, that any state professing to render a democratic service through efficient government will seek to include all of its departmental efforts in its scientific methods, rather than only a part. Public welfare, therefore, may no longer be neglected in the program of any forward-looking state.

Concerning the second conclusion, namely, that the majority of states have undertaken some form of organization, there is need only to refer to the summary and to call attention to common omissions and deficiencies. Preceding chapters give the best summaries that have been made and interpret the present conditions clearly in terms of historical backgrounds and present tendencies. However, one must not hasten to the conclusion that all states save three, Mississippi, Nevada and Utah, have established definite forms of organization dealing with public welfare activities. From further study, it is clear that many other states do not have adequate organized departments such as would be considered a minimum essential in public education, public health, public finance and other departments. The wide variation will be noted below; suffice it to note here that less than half of the states have established complete departmental organizations that go beyond the accidental and partial system represented by the necessary minimum service of some sort of board of supervision or control as it relates to institutions only. Many of these boards include educational institutions. It is noteworthy, however, that practically every state is on record for a better and more comprehensive and economical organization and that few, if any, of those whose departments are not organized, consider the present plan anything more than a step in the right direction. Twelve states have definitely adopted the term "public welfare" and a number of others are setting the stage for reorganization, looking toward the establishment of a department of public welfare. Everywhere there is desire and tendency toward improvement. The National Conference for Social Work, state conferences for social work, and other agencies, including those for the improvement of national and local government, are joining in the movement. That results will be forthcoming there can be no doubt.

Examination of the data already presented will serve to show the remarkable variation in the different states. In addition to the summaries, however, there are certain other factors that need to be emphasized. Even where states adopt the same terminology for their departments there is wide divergence in practice and form of organization. Indeed no two states approximate the same methods or organization. Were it not a fact, and were it not self-evident that social organization in relation to government tends to grow up through accidental methods and forms, the student of public welfare would be loath to believe that such divergence could exist in a nation whose objectives include effective government looking toward broad services economically rendered.

The different designations for state activities, as expressed in the form of boards or departments are as follows:

Charities and Corrections
Charities and Reform
Charities and Probation
Charities
Aid and Charities
Charities and Public Welfare
Public Welfare
Child Welfare
Boards of Control
Boards of Administration
Commissioners of State Institutions
Board of Control and Economy
Directors of State Institutions
Department of Institutions and Agencies
Commission on Penal and Charitable Institutions
Children's Guardians.

To this diversity of terminology should be added the hundreds of different names, terms, types, functions already described.

Alongside these differences should be placed the similar or larger variations such as are found in the dual, overlapping or conflicting boards or commissions within the larger boards. Examples are: A board of children's guardians and a state board of mothers' aid within a state board of charities and correction; a bureau of child and animal protection in a state where a board of

charities and reform performs its work separately; a department of public welfare that has to
do solely with public health; a board of charities
and reform with control over the state fair and
its work; a department of public welfare having
charge of both public health and the usual public
charities and others similar in scope and organization.

It would be expected, therefore, that the specific
duties and activities of the several boards, directors, commissions, departments and bureaus would
vary as widely as the designations of their activities. Such is the case. The story of the varying
activities of the state departments would fill many
pages and make a study all in itself. A state like
New York provides in its legislation for some
eleven duties with reference to its institutions,
after which it proceeds to add still other eleven,
made necessary in the detail of organization and
in the omission of other state departments. Other
states are not different. From the usual inspection, visiting and supervision of institutions, they
vary to the planning, erection and maintenance of
buildings, the making of elaborate reports, the
gathering of statistics, the performing of research. They plan jails and county homes; they
coöperate with state boards; they supervise or
maintain mothers' aid; they look after probation
and the juvenile courts; they direct community
recreation; they enforce compulsory attendance

laws; they look after child labor; they organize to prevent vice and immorality; they even train teachers for special classes; they coöperate in the placement of children; they place out children; they follow up the work of children's homes; they work out new social legislation; they take over the miscellaneous duties and "leftovers" of democratic governmental service. They range from minimum services relating to the old charities and correction to larger activities including county and community organization. They range from the usual care of the dependent, defective and delinquent to the supervision of a state fair and the direction of a state system of athletics. They range from activities looking solely toward the improvement of the conditions of the socially deficient to activities in which all this is omitted and all efforts are directed toward the improvement of the conditions of those who are sick and physically deficient.

It is very clear, however, that in all the efforts set forth through organized state departments there are certain functions and activities that tend to be common to all states, or about which there is common agreement:

1. The general field of child welfare.

2. Certain specific aspects of child welfare, such as child placing or the licensing of children's homes.

3. The general supervision of institutions caring for the socially deficient.

4. Certain specific matters relating to organization, methods and financing in institutions.

5. The general field of "charities and corrections."

6. A central board of supervision or control.

7. A departmental organization under the direction of this board.

Although there may appear similar tendencies in the different states in relation to a number of aspects of the work not mentioned above, in actual practice the topics mentioned are about all that can be found to denote agreement even in general policy and function.   It is possible, however, from the study of present situations and present tendencies to come to definite agreement upon certain principles and policies which ought to obtain in all the states.

Some of the most important considerations underlying the effective state department of public welfare, stated negatively, seem to be:

1. It should not deal with "charities" only.

2. It should not deal with "corrections" only.

3. It should not deal primarily with public education and public health.

4. It should not have to do with "institutions" only.

5. It must not omit constructive and educational programs.

6. It must not be political in its organization.

7. It must not tend to overcentralization.

8. It must not leave out the local units of public welfare.

9. It must not promote overlapping, conflict and inefficiency alongside lack of economy.

10. It must not violate the principles of good government.

Or stated positively there are certain equally self-evident considerations upon which there seems to be possible agreement:

1. It should include the preventive and constructive work of public welfare as well as the old charities and corrections.

2. It should include education, promotion and publicity in its program.

3. It should provide for trained workers and officials experienced in public service.

4. Its state department should supervise all activities within the field of public welfare.

5. Its state department should provide for county units of administration.

6. Its state department should be organized with a view to guaranteeing uniformity and standardization without centralization, either of control of institutions or of purchasing.

7. Its state department should include certain standard bureaus or divisions of work.

8. Its state department should be the actual working administrative unit, rather than the state board.

9. But the state department should be under the general supervision of a non-partisan state board.

10. The state executive officer should be elected by the state board and other officials appointed by this officer, with the approval of the board.

11. The state department should be so organized as to adapt itself to the particular state needs and to conform to the organiaztion of other departments.

12. The state department should, therefore, vary to the extent of taking over the miscellaneous public service and general welfare activities omitted in the other departments of state.

13. Within these limits there should be uniformity of designation, organization and administration that shall conform to good government.

14. This designation and organization should include "public welfare" in the sense designated in this volume; it should allow for separate departments of public health, public education, agriculture and the other state departments agreed upon; and it should work in close coöperation and correlation with all such departments.

The next step, it would seem, is to be found in the working out of a general plan upon which state departments of public welfare which are to be organized, and those already organized, may utilize to the best effect. Such a standard ought to evolve gradually through the processes that are now going on. Such a standard, furthermore, should not be more difficult, either in plan or execution, than the state department of education now beginning to work effectively in all the states. There need be no more difficulty in the way of making the necessary adaptations or of permitting desired variations in the several states than there is in the way of any other local adaptations of departments of government or civic endeavor. Much depends upon the historical background, the present organization, and the local needs and tendencies. If Massachusetts wishes to include town planning and housing in the department of public welfare, it is well that it should; it is doing effective work. Another state might prefer to include housing under the department of health or of safety. If North Carolina wishes to utilize its county superintendents of public welfare for the enforcement of the school-attendance law through family case work and the regular legal avenues, but prefers to leave the work of the rehabilitation of its physically handicapped adults to the vocational division of its state department of education, then this is a good arrangement and a satisfactory exchange of services. Similar variations will always be necessary and there is no desire on the part of anyone to suggest an inflexible type of state department of public welfare to which all states should conform. It is possible, however, within the limitations set forth to work out a very satisfactory and effective type of departmental organization for all states.

Until such a type of state department of public welfare has been worked out more completely and published, the following general requirements should offer the basis for effective work. In general, the departmental organization should tend to conform to that of state departments of education, the country over. Further than this, a combination of the North Carolina plan and the Pennsylvania plan offers perhaps the most satisfactory basis within the present state systems in operation. To these would be added special features taken from other state departments and from these would be taken perhaps features that may prove ineffective. Certain it is that both state systems can be improved and it ought to be the desire of each succeeding state to achieve a more perfect organization of its public welfare departments than has been hitherto developed. The minimum essentials for such improvement would seem to be:

1. Each state should have a State Board of Public Welfare, appointed by the Governor of the State.

2. Each state should have a Department of Public Welfare within this Board of Public Welfare.

3. The executive officer of the Department of Public Welfare should be a Commissioner of Public Welfare.

4. The Commissioner of Public Welfare should be a trained leader elected by the State Board of Public Welfare.

5. Within the State Department of Public Welfare there should be at least the following bureaus or divisions of work:

a. Bureau of Child Welfare or Children.

b. Bureau of Mental Health or Hygiene.

c. Bureau of Institutional Supervision or Control.

d. Bureau of County or Community Organization.

e. Bureau of Rehabilitation or Restoration.

f. Bureau of Education, Promotion and Publicity.

6. The heads of these bureaus should be appointed by the Commissioner of Public Welfare and confirmed by the State Board of Public Welfare; other members of the staff should be so appointed.

7. The county should be the unit of work out in the state and each county should have a board of public welfare and an executive officer or staff who should be trained social workers.

8. Both the state and county plan should provide for close correlation with voluntary agencies and efforts.

9. Each state will, therefore, probably need to combine and reduce and unify certain of its pres-

ent boards and departments, at the same time that it enlarges its total activities.

10. The entire plan should provide that the state department so organized or perfected will conform to the growing tendency toward better organized central government through effective departments that permit of greater economy and of greater local control in all details of democratic service.

It is difficult to find any valid objections to the enactment of the minimum standards set forth above. There are difficulties to be overcome, but they are less than have been the difficulties that have faced other departments like the Department of Education, or even those that have been encountered in the working out of the supervision and control of institutions and the old charities and corrections. It has been only a little while since county departments of education were incompletely organized and their superintendents were untrained. Even now there are many counties in the United States where county officials give but part time and are untrained for their work. Yet no one is disposed to argue thereby that state and county departments of public education are not attainable. The whole history of public education and its administration is an inspiring example of progress in the effective organization of state and county departments. That public welfare administration must go somewhat in advance of its social constituency is but evidence of its conformity to all social measures, legislation and progress. It may appear a local and temporary difficulty; it is no objection. Finally, the question may be raised: What is the alternative which states shall adopt if not an effective and economical administration of this clearly recognized larger service of government?[1]

[1] This chapter offered in substance in the January 1923 *Annals* of the American Academy of Political and Social Science, pp. 137-143.

CHAPTER VIII

THE PENNSYLVANIA PLAN[1]

IN ORDER to illustrate more adequately the principles and policies of public welfare systems the previous summaries and general descriptive statements will now be supplemented by chapters dealing in more detail with two typical states. Pennsylvania is selected because of its excellent plan of organization, its comprehensive application, and the magnitude of its effective expenditures. North Carolina is selected because of the distinctiveness and excellence of its plan and the small appropriations made for its administration and the relatively small appropriations for its maintenance and permanent improvements. Thus the two states stand, in many respects, as contrasting systems, each having distinctive values and methods, not applicable to the other. Each has elements illustrative of the best in all the systems. This chapter will deal with the Pennsylvania system, while Chapter IX will describe the North Carolina plan.

The most important aspects of public welfare as represented by the Pennsylvania plan, for the purposes of this volume, seem to be:

---

[1] Material for this chapter was provided largely through the report of Dr. Ellen Potter, Secretary of Welfare, and special information sent by Mr. Walter Darlington, special representative.

ORGANIZATION CHART OF THE DEPARTMENT OF WELFARE COMMONWEALTH OF PENNSYLVANIA

THE GENERAL PLAN AND ORGANIZATION
SPECIAL POLICIES
THE EXTENT OF APPROPRIATIONS
DETAILS OF BUREAU ORGANIZATIONS
SPECIAL FEATURES AND WORK
RECENT DEVELOPMENTS.

The present Pennsylvania system is that embodied in the "Department of Welfare" of the Commonwealth of Pennsylvania, which grew out of the Department of Public Welfare created by the Act of Assembly in May 1921. This Department, representing a very advanced social policy in state administration in the field of charities and corrections, combined many of the old agencies and forms:

"The powers and duties of the State Board of Charities, established 1869; the Commission on Lunacy, established 1883; The Prison Labor Commission, established 1915; and the Mothers' Assistance Fund, established 1913, were brought together and coördinated in this law, while to these duties were added the responsibility of inspecting and supervising all institutions and agencies for the care of children."

GENERAL ORGANIZATION

The present Department remains organized into four bureaus including the *Bureau of Children,* the *Bureau of Mental Health,* the *Bureau of Assistance,* and the *Bureau of Restoration.* Something of the details of the organization of these bureaus will be described later and may also be ascertained from the accompanying charts. In addition to these service bureaus, the administrative code added to the powers and duties of the Department that of fiscal control of state-owned institutions. As integral units of the Department of Welfare, therefore, are the following:

Penal and Correctional Institutions
    Eastern State Penitentiary
    Western State Penitentiary
    Pennsylvania Industrial Reformatory
    State Industrial Home for Women
    Pennsylvania Training School.

Home for Afflicted Soldiers and Sailors
    Pennsylvania Soldiers and Sailors' Home.

Mental Hospitals
    Allentown State Hospital
    Danville State Hospital
    Farview State Hospital
    Harrisburg State Hospital
    Norristown State Hospital
    Warren State Hospital
    Wernersville State Hospital
    Torrance State Hospital.

Medical and Surgical Hospitals
    Ashland State Hospital
    Blossburg State Hospital
    Coaldale State Hospital
    Connellsville State Hospital
    Hazleton State Hospital
    Nanticoke State Hospital

Philipsburg State Hospital
Scranton State Hospital
Shamokin State Hospital
Locust Mountain Hospital.
Institutions for Feeble-Minded and Epileptic
Pennhurst State School
Polk State School
Laurelton State Village.

DEPARTMENTAL POLICIES

The statement of the general policies of the department made by Dr. Potter provides an excellent standard for the consideration of all public welfare work. The development of the Pennsylvania Department during its recent years has been based upon these principles quoted from Dr. Potter's report:

First—Major emphasis should be placed upon education of the public, Boards of Trustees and Superintendents rather than on such police powers as the law might give in the effort to improve standards of scientific work, social service or business management in various fields.

Second—That the principle of "home rule in welfare work" should be recognized as fundamental and that local responsibility and initiative should be encouraged in all social activities whether conducted by private charity or public officials.

Third—That the Department should so develop its organization that it should be ready at all times and in all places to render expert consultation and advisory service to communities, organizations and individuals throughout the State in all matters relating to professional work or institutional administration.

THE PENNSYLVANIA BIENNIAL APPROPRI-
ATIONS FOR WELFARE ADMINISTRATION
AND INSTITUTIONS

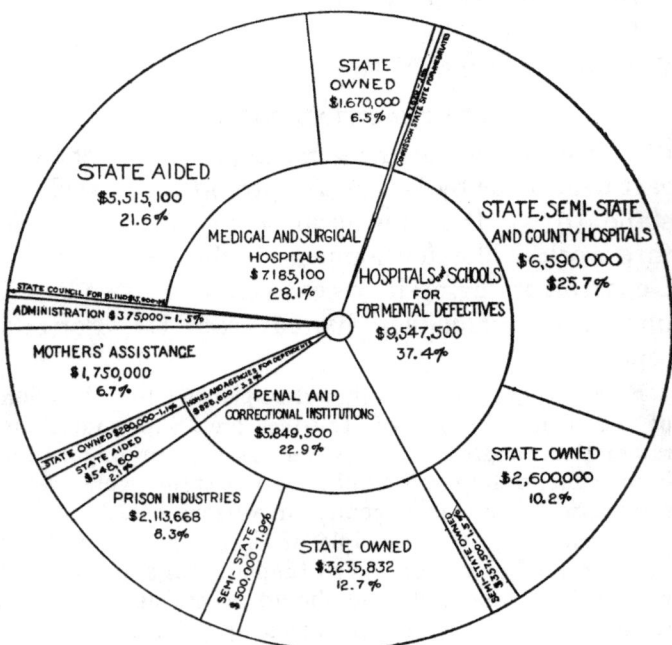

STATE
OWNED
$1,670,000
6.5%

CONTROL-STATE GIFT FOR INEBRIATES

STATE AIDED
$5,515,100
21.6%

STATE, SEMI-STATE
AND COUNTY HOSPITALS
$6,590,000
$25.7%

MEDICAL AND SURGICAL
HOSPITALS
$7,185,100
28.1%

HOSPITALS & SCHOOLS
FOR
FOR MENTAL DEFECTIVES
$9,547,500
37.4%

STATE COUNCIL FOR BLIND $5,000

ADMINISTRATION $375,000 – 1.5%

MOTHERS' ASSISTANCE
$1,750,000
6.7%

HOMES AND AGENCIES FOR DEFECTIVES
$808,000 – 3.3%

PENAL AND
CORRECTIONAL INSTITUTIONS
$5,849,500
22.9%

STATE OWNED $250,000 – 1.1%

STATE AIDED
$548,600
2.1%

STATE OWNED
$2,600,000
10.2%

PRISON INDUSTRIES
$2,113,668
8.3%

SEMI-STATE
$500,000 – 1.9%

STATE OWNED
$3,235,832
12.7%

SEMI-STATE OWNED $6,257,000 – 24.5%

TOTAL $25,558,329

Fourth—That in the re-interpretation of the laws under which the Department operates the emphasis should always be placed upon the *prevention* of the conditions which have created the necessity for public and private welfare activities, namely, the *Prevention of Poverty, the Prevention of Delinquency, the Prevention of Crime,* and *the Prevention of Mental Disease and Defect.*

APPROPRIATIONS AND SCOPE

The extent of services rendered by the Pennsylvania Department of Welfare may be seen at a glance from the accompanying chart showing the total amount and distribution of state welfare funds in Pennsylvania for the biennium beginning June 1, 1925, and ending May 31, 1927, the latest legislative appropriation. The general summaries may be seen from the following table:

WELFARE APPROPRIATION BIENNIUM 1925-27

Distribution	Amount	Per Cent
Administration	$ 375,000	1.5
State Council for Blind	15,000	.1 +
Mothers' Assistance	1,750,000	6.7
Homes and Agencies for Dependents	828,600	3.2
Penal and Correctional Institutions	5,849,500	22.9
Hospitals and Schools for Mental Defectives	9,547,500	37.4
Medical and Surgical Hospitals	7,185,100	28.1
Total	$25,558,329	100.0

Special Staff. In addition to the heads of bureaus with their respective staffs, it became evi-

dent as the work of the Department developed
that there were certain common functions which
needed specialists in which all bureaus might be
served alike and in which the public institutions
might coöperate. A special staff was therefore
planned and employed, to include:

Supervisor of Institutional Management

A General Accountant

A Consulting Engineer

A Nutrition Supervisor

A Social Service Consultant

An Agriculturist.

The functions of these are perhaps largely self-
explanatory. The supervision of nutrition and
institution management have been especially important in bringing about great savings and better
management with the accompanying better nutrition, good health and morale.

Social Service. Concerning the social service
consultant, established in accordance with the Department's policy to find for family case work a
person of wide experience, in an effort to convert
the Directors of the Poor and Hospital Executives
to the need of trained family case workers, Dr.
Potter says:

"We were fortunate beyond our expectations in securing as Consultant one who not only was equipped in family
case work by years of experience in the Charity Organization Society of Philadelphia, but experienced in hospital
social service which she had organized and developed in

the Pennsylvania Hospital, Philadelphia, and in addition had still further developed her experience in work for dependent children.

"We have, therefore, been able to make friendly contacts with the Directors of the Poor in various counties; we have been able to make practical demonstrations of the uses of trained service in handling their problems and we have had the pleasure of seeing some of them converted to the idea of employing their own trained workers.

"In addition to service to the Directors of the Poor service has been rendered to our State mental and general hospitals. The chief need in the mental hospitals has been personnel properly trained to handle the very difficult problem of social work in these special institutions, the superintendents being alive to the need. In our general hospitals the greatest need is to convert the administrators of some of these institutions to the advantages and economies of trained social service for their patients.

"The third function to be performed by the Consultant is in connection with the development of hospital social service in State-aided hospitals and will be discussed more fully in its relation to the activities of the Bureau of Assistance."

Research. An important part of the Department is that of the research and statistical unit in which a number of studies have been made and others are under way or being planned. Among the topics included in social research are:

Poor Law Administration
Adoptions in Pennsylvania
Modern Methods of Training Delinquent Girls
Mothers' Aid Cases
Inter-Racial Problems.

Poor Law Administration. Concerning the poor law administration, the Pennsylvania policy is of educational value. Says the report:

Convinced, as we are, that public welfare work must be built up upon a local sense of social responsibility we have made a study in very considerable detail of the costs and methods of local care of the poor, which by law is vested, as we believe it should be, in our poor law officials known as Directors in the county and Overseers in the townships.

Very few of our citizens realize what important functions are lodged with our county government in caring for the needy and distressed. This is most easily reflected in their taxation for poor relief. In the ten-year period, 1914-1923, our 67 counties raised $95,000,000 for poor relief purposes. In 1922, the last year for which complete figures are available, our counties spent $5,000,000 on the maintenance of their almshouses; they gave more than $1,000,000 in outdoor relief; and with a number of smaller items the aggregate expenditures for the relief of the poor were nearly $10,000,000.

It must be clear that in order to have such large monetary outlays go as far as possible in the alleviation of poverty only the most efficient modern methods should be employed and the strictest economy be observed. It cannot be said that Pennsylvania at the present moment is utilizing her opportunities to the utmost in this respect. One reason for it is our slowly changing conceptions of what poor relief ought to be. The chief hindrance, however, is the multiplicity of our poor laws—many enacted decades ago for special purposes which have long since become inoperative.

Perhaps the most serious fact to be observed in connection with poor relief is that no effort is made by many of the local officials to prevent poverty and to rehabilitate families by constructive family case work, and their failure to interpret the laws under which they operate in the light of modern social understanding is a real stumbling-block to their own progress.

The most important instruments through which we are caring for our indigent poor are our 83 almshouses or poor farms varying in size to accommodate from 1 to over 1,000 persons; exhibiting wide differences in equipment and administration. These almshouses report a value of land, building and equipment of over $16,000,000 and own over 17,000 acres of land of which more than 10,000 were reported to be under cultivation.

To support an average of more than 8,000 poor in our almshouses in 1922 we spent over $2,000,000 on their direct maintenance and expended almost $3,000,000 on our almshouse administration. It took over 1,000 paid employees to look after the inmates of our almshouses.

Originally the idea of the almshouse or poor farm was to have the inmates through their work on the farm bear a share of their maintenance. In more recent years the type of inmate has changed, however, and LESS THAN 10% were reported to be able-bodied in 1922, and it is obvious that the farms can no longer be run with inmate labor. (In two counties at least this has been obviated by the able-bodied labor of the inmates of the county prisons—Berks and Dauphin Counties.)

Pennsylvania's almshouses show a considerable decrease in the number of inmates in the last few decades, and a decided change in the relation of the almshouse population to the general population. In 1904 the United States census enumerates for Pennsylvania 133.2 almshouse inmates per 100,000 population. This ratio has decreased to 125.3 in 1910 and still further decreased to 89.6 in 1923. The corresponding ratios for the almshouse population per 100,000 of the population of the United States as a whole were 100.0 in 1904, 91.5 in 1910 and 71.5 in 1923.

These figures show a relatively greater decrease in the almshouse population in relation to Pennsylvania's population than is the case if all the almshouse inmates in the United States are considered in relation to the population of the country, but even *Pennsylvania, in proportion to her population, has more inmates in her almshouses than has the country at large.*

An important function of our county poor relief administration is the giving of "Outdoor Relief," that is, chiefly to supplement an insufficient income through grants in groceries and other aid in kind. Thus in 1922 more than 56,000 received outdoor relief—about 6,000 men, 15,000 women, and 35,000 children. The types which constitute this army dependent upon poor relief are mainly the following:

1. Widows with dependent children and the wives (with dependent children) of husbands confined in institutions for the mentally sick.

2. The "industrial poor" which means that the dependency of the bread winner is traceable more or less directly to industrial causes.

3. The poverty traceable to some moral turpitude on the part of the bread winner, such as desertion, incarceration, etc.

4. The aged dependents.

Though there are notable exceptions, the giving of outdoor relief generally is not done as efficiently and constructively as it might be. In most cases, aid is given without a definite plan of budgeting the families' needs nor is it done with an eye looking toward their quick rehabilitation as self-supporting citizens.

Illustrations can be multiplied from the official records of persons receiving grants of money, grocery orders, etc., years on end, long after the emergency for which the original grant was given has ceased; families, unto the third generation, are "on the county"; persons are given allowances who are not in need and a study of the actual amounts given in truly needy cases all too often indicates that the sum is not sufficient to be of constructive service and so the *tax-payers' money is actually wasted.*

A Recommended Policy. The forward-looking poor relief program which the Department would recommend would include:

The county as a unit of poor relief administration
Consolidation of smaller counties for poor relief purposes
Clearer recognition of the changing type of almshouse
  population
Outdoor relief, coupled with supervisory social service
Employment of paid, well trained poor relief officers
Recognition of close relation between dependency and
  social and industrial situations.

BUREAU ACTIVITIES

The Bureau of Children, in addition to working out many details of legal duties, the holding of conferences, coöperating in special studies and publications, has the following very definite duties:

Supervision over
  Institutions for care of dependent children
  Institutions for training of delinquent children
  Child-caring agencies
  Day nurseries
Administration of Mothers' Assistance fund
Consultation on community child welfare plans and probation service

Administration of importation law
Licensing boarding homes for infants (act of
(1925)
Conduct of educational programs on methods
of child care.

Other special work includes a *mothers' assistance
section* and under the supervision of the assistant
director of the Bureau of Children, special institutions for *juvenile delinquents.*

Bureau of Assistance. The Bureau of Assistance, in addition to special inspection and surveys,
the study of progressive methods and principles,
coöperation in research and publication, has the
following functions:

Supervision over
    State-aided hospitals
    State-aided homes for adults
    County almshouses
    City, township and district poorhouses
Certification of agencies soliciting funds
Representation of the Department in disasters
from floods, etc.
Administration of State aid to private hospitals
and homes.

Of special interest is the work of four field representatives who are trained and experienced hospital social workers who render special service and
bring the hospitals into touch with the social resources of their communities. Similar emphasis is
placed upon the need for constructive family and

individual case work and coöperation with other state departments in working out adjustments of family cases.

Bureau of Mental Health. One of the recent advances made in the Bureau of Mental Health is the employment of a field psychiatrist devoting more of his time to clinic and community service. Special emphasis is placed upon community service and there are now 41 clinics, with more to be established. The functions of the Bureau of Mental Health include:

Supervision over
> Mental hospitals, state, county and private
> Institutions for epileptics
> Institutions for feeble-minded
> Mental clinics

Administration of mental health law
Provision of psychiatric and psychological consultants for correctional institutions
Stimulation of occupational therapy, music and allied activities in institutions
Provision of community supervision and group surveys of mental patients.

Bureau of Restoration. Special problems have been encountered in the Bureau of Restoration, including the chaotic administration and inadequate housing in state and county prisons, the abolition of the fee system, development of regional state farms, together with other standard problems of modern penology. The duties of the Bureau of Restoration include:

Supervision over
   Penitentiaries
   Reformatory
   County jails
   Municipal prison
   Borough jails
Assembling of criminal statistics
Conduct of prison industries
Superintendence of transfer of prisoners.

A special section on prison labor as shown in the accompanying chart completes the general organization of the Bureau of Restoration.

Community Welfare Organization. One of the chief interests of the Department is that of community welfare organization and community service. The county plan of organization has not been satisfactorily worked out in a sufficient number of cases. Much progress, however, has been made and the outlook is promising. Dr. Potter says:

The need of developing a county consciousness for the social welfare of the handicapped groups in those communities was very early felt. The wide breach frequently found between the poor law officials of a county and the philanthropic public, largely due to misunderstanding of aims and purposes, made it imperative that the Department should endeavor to bring about mutual understanding and coöperative effort. To that end a Field Representative was appointed to promote this undertaking.

The work of this representative is educational, coöperative and promotive. Numerous calls for his services have been received and we believe that as a result there is developing in many of our counties a definite sense of social responsibility and a keen appreciation of problems to be solved.

The present-day trend in official charitable work is away from the Pennsylvania system with its paid directors and overseers of the poor and toward the appointment of unpaid boards of trustees who employ full-time trained service to carry out their policies.

We do not believe that the people of Pennsylvania have as yet come to the point of wishing to change their traditional policy and we do not recommend it but we do believe that the time has come for more complete understanding between public and private charity and more effective coöperation if the costs of this charity are to be kept within bounds.

The Department during the past year has been able to render considerable service to many communities which were studying their own problems.

The great mass of statistical material relating to charities which is in our files is at the disposal of the City and State Chambers of Commerce and is frequently consulted by them and by Community Chests and Welfare organizations.

We are also able to render special consultation service on social, accounting, nursing, engineering and other problems.

RECENT DEVELOPMENTS

Among the most important developments of the last year and the new legislature are a number of new laws and appropriations with reference to specific institutions, such as Torrance State Hospital, Laureton Village, Muncy Farms, and Rockview and Eastern Penitentiaries

The State General Hospitals for new building and maintenance

Three new laws marking advance in prison labor matters

The abolition of the sheriff's fee in certain counties

Two new acts sponsored by the Children's Commission governing adoptions and bringing infant boarding houses under regulation by the Welfare Department

A continuation of the Children's Commission

Authority for the appointment of a commission for the study of prison parole

The establishment of a State Council for the blind in the Department of Welfare, to include the Secretary of Welfare, Superintendent of Public Instruction, the Secretary of Labor and Industry, and four others to be appointed by the Governor.

A new law to check improper collection of moneys by irresponsible organizations

Voting of a lump sum of one million dollars to the Department of Welfare for general medical and surgical treatment of the indigent

An amendment to the mental health act of 1923

The Arow law for identification of babies in maternity institutions by foot-prints

The Guerin law, under which juries may specify capital punishment or life imprisonment in first-degree murder cases. Under the old law capital punishment was mandatory

An amendment to authorize the loan of fifty million dollars to complete state building program, to be approved by the next legislature and then submitted to popular vote.

Finally the charts on the following pages will give a comprehensive picture of the entire Pennsylvania plan.

CHAPTER IX

THE NORTH CAROLINA PLAN[1]

THE present system of public welfare in North Carolina has had a rather unusual development in that it did not evolve slowly and gradually over a long period of time. It is true that provisions for the old system were of long standing, but the new system grew up rapidly in what was, as far as public welfare was concerned, practically a sleeping state. It was thus some time before North Carolina really understood what had been opened up to it. The old North Carolina Board of Public Charities which preceded the new system existed from 1868 until 1917, but it had functioned only in a limited way, and thus can hardly be regarded as a step in the development of the present system. During this time, however, a small group of interested citizens, headed by "the father of public welfare in North Carolina," A. W. McAlister, of Greensboro, had been conferring and planning for some time before the new plan materialized, and its materialization was due to their plans and efforts. But the transformation was sudden and so sweeping and the new plan so big that it caused as much comment abroad as it did at home.

---

[1] Most of the material in this chapter was provided by Commissioner Kate Burr Johnson and Miss Nell Battle Lewis.

As a result of the efforts of these interested citizens in obtaining the support of various organizations and groups, the Legislature of 1917 passed the state-wide public welfare act. The State Board of Charities and Public Welfare was created with powers and duties larger than those of the old North Carolina Board of Public Charities. The county commissioners were given power to create county boards of public welfare and also to elect a county superintendent of public welfare. The law as it related to the counties was purely permissive and only two counties were organized for the work at that time.

It was in the Legislature of 1919 that the mandatory act was passed which caused the organization of every county in the state for public welfare. A county board of public welfare consisting of three persons was appointed in every county. In counties of 25,000 or over (later amended to read 32,000) a superintendent of public welfare was required. In all other counties where the commissioners failed to elect, the superintendent of schools was required to serve as ex-officio superintendent of public welfare. The state-wide juvenile court act was passed creating a juvenile court in every county with the clerk of the Superior Court as judge. Thus, the machinery was created by which the whole program of public welfare in the state could be carried on.

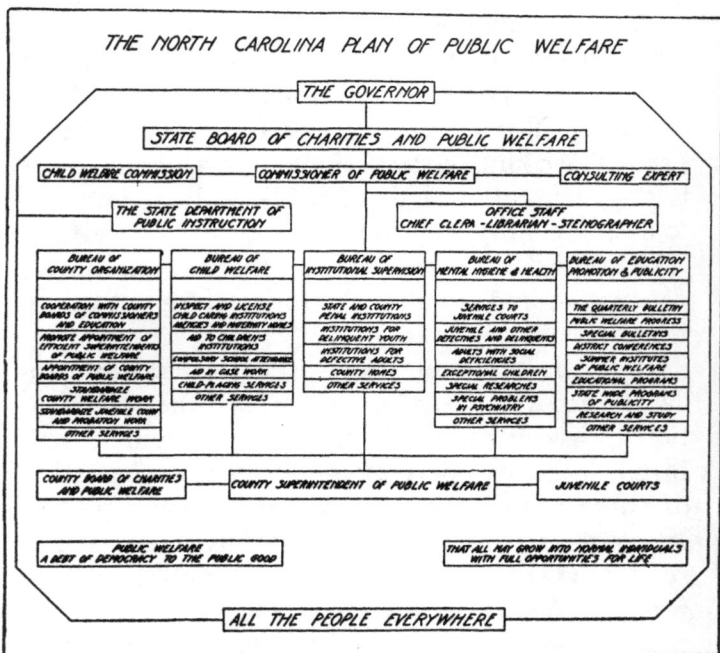

THE NORTH CAROLINA PLAN OF PUBLIC WELFARE

Compare the North Carolina organization with Pennsylvania.

The North Carolina Board of Charities and Public Welfare is composed of seven members, two of whose terms expire each two years and who serve without pay. They are appointed by the Governor and confirmed by the Legislature. This board in turn appoints a Commissioner of Public Welfare who is the executive officer of the board. The work of the board has been divided into five bureaus to carry out the duties and requirements of the board under the law.

COUNTY ORGANIZATION

Coöperation with county boards of commissioners and education
Promote appointment of efficient superintendents of public welfare
Appointment of county boards of public welfare
Standardize county welfare work
Standardize juvenile court and probation work
Compulsory school attendance
Other services.

INSTITUTIONAL SUPERVISION

State and county penal institutions
Outdoor Poor Relief
County Homes
Other services.

CHILD WELFARE

Administration of Mothers' Aid
Inspect and license child-caring institutions,

THE NORTH CAROLINA COUNTY PLAN OF PUBLIC WELFARE

agencies and maternity homes
Aid to children's institutions
Supervision of institutions for children
Aid in case work
Child-placing services
Other services.

MENTAL HEALTH AND HYGIENE

Services to juvenile courts
Juvenile and other defectives and delinquents
Adults with social deficiencies
Exceptional children
Inspection of state and private institutions for
the mentally defective and the insane
Special problems in psychopathology
Other services.

PROMOTION AND PUBLICITY

Public Welfare Progress
Special bulletins
Programs for coöperating organizations
Summer institutes of public welfare
News and feature stories to newspapers
Other services.

The State Superintendent of Public Instruction,
the State Health Officer, and the Commissioner
of Public Welfare form a State Child Welfare
Commission, whose duty it is to enforce the child
labor laws, the law providing for seats in certain
mercantile and manufacturing plants, and the

sanitary regulations. The county superintendent of public welfare is the authorized local agent of this commission.

Just as the State has a well organized plan with its department and bureaus functioning each in its own special field, so the North Carolina plan provides for a county unit with similar definite functions. If we classify the duties of the county superintendent of public welfare in a way similar to the above bureau division we should have the following:

COUNTY ADMINISTRATION AND STATE
COÖPERATION

To maintain an office and keep all records necessary for the success of the work
To act as secretary of the county board
To act as agent for the state board
To inspect county institutions, jails, convict camps
To act as agent of the child welfare commission.

GENERAL CHILD WELFARE WORK

To look after the child in danger of dependency, delinquency or neglect
To exercise oversight of children placed out by the state or placing agencies

To look after all other needs of children and youth in the county

To give aid to families wherever expedient.

RELIEF

To investigate relief cases and advise as to expenditure of poor funds

To supervise and help persons discharged from hospitals for insane, state prisons or other institutions

To help the unemployed find work

To study conditions and sources of poverty.

PROBATION AND JUVENILE COURT WORK

To act as chief probation officer for delinquent youth and to become the guardian of children in need of guidance

To develop the system of juvenile courts

To act as chief probation officer where there is more than one

To study conditions and sources of delinquency.

SCHOOL ATTENDANCE WORK

To act as chief school attendance officer

To lead families to appreciate education and coöperate with the school

To enforce the compulsory education law dealing with cases beyond the control of the school officials

To coöperate with school officials.

COMMUNITY ORGANIZATION

To assist in correlating all community agencies
To encourage organization of other needed volunteer agencies
To enforce laws relating to amusement places
To promote wholesome recreation for the community.

THE PRESENT COUNTY ORGANIZATIONS

The following figures give the organization of the State in regard to public welfare work as of November, 1924:

Whole-time Superintendents 45
Part-time Superintendents 10
Superintendents of schools serving 45
                                                                   ———
                                                                   100

Of the 55 counties included in the first two items 29 are mandatory because of population and two are mandatory by special statute, showing at least fourteen full-time superintendents in counties where it is not mandatory.

Of the fifty-five superintendents of public welfare, thirty-seven have attended college, twenty-seven have college degrees, and the great majority have attended the summer institutes for public welfare at the University of North Carolina. Thirty-two have been teachers, and three are ministers of the gospel, while fifty-three are church members. The average age is thirty-seven years. Fourteen of the superintendents have been in public welfare work since the new North Carolina system was installed. Twenty-nine had done some sort of community work previous to entering the field of public welfare. Few, however, had professional training for social work in the technical sense of the word, except as received at summer session at the University Institutes.

A summary of the efforts of these superintendents, however, will show something, both of the difficulties and successes that have attended their efforts.

SUMMARY OF WORK DONE BY COUNTY ORGANIZA-
TIONS DURING THE YEAR 1924, FOR THE
ENTIRE STATE[2]

Total Official Cases Handled.................... 2881
    (a) Number placed on probation....... 1092
    (b) Number placed in private homes....   564
    (c) Number placed in institutions......   446
    (d) Number otherwise disposed of.....   488
    (e) Number of cases dismissed........   291
Total Unofficial Cases Handled................ 3128
    (a) Number of children handled through
        parents 1444
    (b) Number of children placed in private
        homes   257
    (c) Number of children placed in institu-
        tions   138
    (d) Number reprimanded and warned..   828
    (e) Number of cases otherwise settled..   461

---

[2] From the Report of the Commissioner, 1923-25.

School Attendance Records:
- (a) Number of children reported for
      non-attendance 41191
- (b) Number of children returned to school.... 23704
- (c) Number of prosecutions for non-attendance   636
- (d) Number of visits to schools by officers.... 4950

Poor Fund:
- (a) Number of applications investigated...... 1848
- (b) Number placed on list..................   599
- (c) Number removed from list..............   398
- (d) Number placed on County Home list......   448

Total Conferences Held...................... 19302
- (a) Number of Board member
      conferences 1222
- (b) Number of Juvenile Court Judge
      conferences 2854
- (c) Number of general conferences..... 15226

Total Meetings   715
- (a) Number of Board Meetings........   198
- (b) Number of general meetings.......   517

Total Investigations 2425
- (a) Number of Mothers' Aid..........   789
- (b) Number of family............... 1636

Total Inspections 3548
- (a) Number of jail..................   429
- (b) Number of road camp............   244
- (c) Number of County Homes........   738
- (d) Number of Factory..............   979
- (e) Number of Store................. 1158

Total Certificates 7096
- (a) Number of age.................. 6036
- (b) Number of employment........... 1060

Total Parole Work........................... 2605
- (a) Children 2230
- (b) Adults   375

Miscellaneous Items:
- (a) Number of home visits.................. 17606
- (b) Number of office calls.................. 26314

(c) Number of persons advised.............. 14289
(d) Number of active Mothers' Aid cases..... 222
(e) Number of Adults prosecuted............ 558
(f) Number of letters mailed................ 30975
(g) Number of 'phone calls................. 34308
(h) Number of miles traveled...............263669
(i) Number of trips outside of county........ 1139
(j) Number of investigations for Agencies.... 1654

INSTITUTIONAL SUPERVISION AND WORK

One of the most difficult of all the problems of the State Board of Charities and Public Welfare is that of coöperating with the larger state institutions of public welfare, with the needed amount of supervision and coöperation on the one hand and the minimum amount of direction and control on the other. The institutional problem is a many-sided one and each institution has its own peculiar problems resulting from the type of person served, the location from which the population is drawn, and the amount of financial and moral support given it.

There are two types of county institutions in some sections of North Carolina that are becoming less and less a necessity and more and more a useless burden on the tax-payer. These are the county homes and the county jails which should be replaced by district homes and district jails. In proportion to the increase in the general population of this state, the population of county homes has been steadily decreasing for thirty years. A number of county homes have only a few inmates.

One county home at present has only one. A number of county jails stand vacant or have only a few prisoners annually. Such institutions are a useless burden on the tax-payers when their function could be accomplished more efficiently and with less expense by district institutions.

Prisons and Prison Problems: Organization of the Citizens' Committee of One Hundred in 1922 was one of the most significant forward steps that have been taken in prison reform in North Carolina. This committee is composed of prominent persons in the State who have declared themselves interested in this subject and desirous of studying prison conditions in North Carolina impartially. The purpose of the committee is to educate the public as to these conditions and the need of prison reform and to promote needed legislation.

In 1922 a survey of county jails and chaingangs in North Carolina was made. A report of this survey which disclosed many conditions needing improvement was made to the Committee of One Hundred and a bulletin containing this report published.

In the General Assembly of 1923, the bills sponsored by the Committee of One Hundred were:

1. To place the State Prison on an appropriation basis.

2. To transfer the criminal insane from the State Prison to the State Hospital for the insane.

3. To abolish flogging and the use of the dark cell.

Of these, the first two were passed and the third defeated.

In April, 1923, prison reform in North Carolina received fresh impetus by the insistence of the State Commissioner of Public Welfare that there should be full investigation of serious charges made against the prison administration. This led to announcement by Governor Morrison of a program of prison reform in which were included:

1. Abolition of flogging and the use of dark cells in the State Prison system.

2. Commutation of the sentences of all state prisoners to "indeterminate," that is, the maximum and minimum terms.

3. Recommendation that the county commissioners abolish flogging in their county systems.

4. Instructions to the solicitors to visit the county jails and chain-gangs in their districts and to report to the Governor on their condition.

A campaign of education on prison reform has been carried on in 1922-24 through "Public Welfare Progress," the monthly publication of the State Board of Charities and Public Welfare.

County Homes: A survey of county homes in North Carolina was made in 1922 by representatives of the State Board of Charities and Public Welfare. Questionnaires were sent and visits and mental examinations made in a group of representative county homes. A special bulletin on Poor Relief in North Carolina showing conditions of county homes has been published by the State Board of Charities and Public Welfare.

The General Assembly of 1923 passed a law permitting two or more counties to unite in building a district home for the indigent. No progress, however, has been made towards the acceptance of this law by the counties.

Twenty-five new county homes have been built since 1919 or are now under construction. With the exception of two, the cost of these has ranged from $20,000 to $175,000. The aggregate cost is $1,000,000. Although all are not of the cottage type, emphasis is being placed on this plan of structure.

In 1921 the number of inmates of county homes in this state was 1,630; in 1922 it was 1,650; in 1923, it was 1,775. However, the number of inmates per 100,000 of the state's population has decreased within every census period for the last thirty years.

The cost of maintenance of county homes exclusive of farm products used in the homes in 1921 was $372,000; in 1922 it was $384,000; and in 1923 it was $403,000.

The cost of maintaining county homes including farm products used in the homes in 1921 was

$584,000.   Estimated for 1922-23,—in 1922 it was $597,000; in 1923 it was $616,000.

The cost of outdoor poor relief, that is, relief of the indigent who are not confined to county homes, in 1921 was $157,000; in 1922 it was $175,000; and in 1923 it was $196,000. It has been found that much money is wasted in outdoor poor relief because of the lack of proper supervision. As provided by law the superintendent of public welfare should supervise this under the county commissioners.

Institutions for Defectives: North Carolina has one institution for the mentally defective, the Caswell Training School at Kinston. This institution was established by the General Assembly of 1911. It now cares for about 350 inmates. The Legislature of 1923 gave the Caswell Training School an appropriation for permanent improvements to bring the school up to a capacity of 400. Insufficient maintenance funds, however, limit the number. There are scores of mentally defective persons on the waiting list of the Caswell Training School which, despite all its efforts, cannot meet the tremendous problem of the feeble-minded in this state.

Hospitals for the Insane: There are three hospitals for the insane in North Carolina with a total capacity of 4,435.

The General Assembly of 1923 provided liberally for these hospitals in comparison with other charitable institutions. The number of insane persons in the state, however, is increasing in proportion to the general population. The hospital for the negro insane at Goldsboro is particularly crowded. Since 1923, provision has been made for buildings at the institutions at Raleigh and Goldsboro to care for the criminal insane who are to be moved from the State Prison where they have been confined.

In addition to those mentioned, the state bureau supervises the various institutions for delinquent youth and the Orthopedic Hospital for Crippled Children. (See Institutions for Children.)

Briefly, the state institutions that come under the supervision of the State Board of Charities and Public Welfare are:

Hospital for the Insane at Raleigh. Established in 1848 through the efforts of Dorothea Dix, who brought about the establishment of hospitals for the insane in 20 states.

State Prison at Raleigh. Established in 1869.

Hospital for the Insane at Morganton. Established in 1875.

Hospital for Negro Insane at Goldsboro. Established in 1880.

Stonewall Jackson Training School for delinquent white boys at Concord. Established in 1909.

North Carolina Orthopedic Hospital for crippled children at Gastonia. Established in 1909.

Caswell Training School for mental defectives at Kinston. Established in 1911.

Samarcand Manor for delinquent white girls at Samarcand. Established in 1917.

Morrison Industrial School for delinquent negro boys in Richmond County. Established by the General Assembly of 1921. Now finished but not opened.

Eastern Carolina Industrial Training School for delinquent white boys at Rocky Mount. Established by the General Assembly of 1923 and opened in 1925.

The State of North Carolina also contributes to the support of the Masonic Orphanage and the Orphanage for Colored Children, both at Oxford. These institutions are also under the supervision of the State Board of Charities and Public Welfare.

This list does not include the county institutions and the private institutions that the State Board supervises.

CHILD WELFARE SUPERVISION AND WORK

The Bureau of Child Welfare has two main divisions, Mothers' Aid and Children's Institutions.

Mothers' Aid: Although North Carolina was the 41st state to pass a Mothers' Aid law it is one of the few states administering the law on a state-wide basis and meeting county appropriations dollar for dollar. The $50,000 granted by the

Legislature of 1923 was apportioned to the counties on a population basis. Fifty-seven counties have active cases. Most of these counties have used their quotas in full or will do so before the 1925 Legislature meets and have mothers waiting for aid. The fund for the 43 counties not taking advantage of their quotas stays in the State Treasury. These quotas cannot be transferred to other counties.

Mothers' Aid is an attempt to provide every child a home with its own mother. The mother in order to be able to receive this financial help from county and state must be a woman of character, ability, and health sufficient to maintain a home and train her children; who has lost her husband by death, desertion, insanity, or crime; who has children under 14 years of age and who lacks sufficient means to care for them. Applications for aid are made through the superintendent of public welfare who, after personal investigation of all available sources of information, submits his findings in writing to his county board of public welfare.

This board is required by law to go into the merits of the case, investigating personally if they so desire, and to refuse the case or approve it, suggesting the sum needed, monthly, by the mother to maintain and improve her standard of living. With the approval of the county board the case goes to the county commissioners who decide upon the amount to be granted.

The case is then forwarded, in duplicate, to the State Board of Charities and Public Welfare. The Director of Mothers' Aid goes over the application carefully and if everything is in order approves the case, returning one copy to the county superintendent for filing. If the information given is not sufficient the State may ask for further information, may offer suggestions as to needed improvements in housing, health, etc., or increase in appropriation.

The average Mothers' Aid family consists of four children, living with a widowed mother 35 years old in a four-room cottage in the country on an appropriation of $19.12 a month, plus milk from her own cow, eggs from her own hens, vegetables, fruits, and meats of her own growing.

A mother with one child can receive a maximum of $15.00 a month; two children, $25.00, and five children, $40.00.

Since the law went into effect 243 mothers have been granted aid. Of these 19 have been removed from the list because of various reasons—nine widows have remarried, two moved out of North Carolina, two for immorality, two because of death, one mother became self-supporting, one deserting husband returned home, one mother secured a belated government pension,—and one secured more aid from another fund than she could get under the state law.

The State Director has visited every county administering Mothers' Aid and has been in two-thirds of the homes. With few exceptions the mothers are fine, capable women.

The great need is more money. More money in the state for individual mothers and for trained visitors to supervise the work, more money in the counties in order that county superintendents of public welfare may have sufficient office help to do their part of the work thoroughly.

Institutions for Dependent Children: It is the duty of the State Board of Charities and Public Welfare to license and visit duly approved public and private institutions caring for children. It also refuses to license any that are not properly established and well-equipped to receive and care for children.

At present there are twenty-two private and two semi-private orphanages in the state. The semi-private are the white and colored orphanages at Oxford, both of which receive state appropriation.

During the year ending June, 1924, the orphanages of North Carolina cared for 3,618 children. There will be some increase in this number in another year as three of the institutions are enlarging their plants.

The Children's Home Society of North Carolina places children in foster homes with a view to permanent placement and adoption. This does not take place until the family and the child have had an opportunity of living together long enough to determine whether adoption would be satisfactory.

Following is a list of child-caring institutions in North Carolina:

Alexander Home, Charlotte.
Baptist Orphanage and Kennedy Home, Thomasville.
Buncombe County Children's Home, Asheville.
Catholic Orphanage, Nazareth.
Christian Orphanage, Elon College.
Eliada Orphanage, Asheville.
Falcon Orphanage, Falcon.
Freewill Baptist Orphanage, Middlesex.
Grandfather Orphans' Home, Banner Elk.
I. O. O. F. Home, Goldsboro.
Juvenile Relief Home, Winston-Salem.
Memorial School (Colored), Winston-Salem.
Methodist Protestant Children's Home, High Point.
Methodist Orphanage, Raleigh.
Mountain Orphanage, Black Mountain.
Nazareth Orphanage, Crescent.
Oxford Orphanage, Oxford.
Oxford Orphanage (Colored), Oxford.
Presbyterian Orphans' Home, Barium Springs.

Pythian Home, Clayton.
St. Ann's Orphanage, Belmont.
Thompson Orphanage, Charlotte.
Wright Refuge, Durham.
North Carolina Children's Home Society, Greensboro.

Institutions for Delinquents: There are two institutions supported by the state that care for delinquents. These schools are correctional in their nature, their efforts being directed toward constructive ends. In addition to the regular work in the elementary grades and high school, special emphasis is given to vocational training.

The Jackson Training School, Concord: This school established in 1909 receives boys under sixteen years of age from the juvenile courts. It is supported entirely by the state, although counties and organizations have erected cottages. Twelve cottages are now in use and two more ready for occupancy as soon as sufficient funds for maintenance are available. These cottages approximate the family home in that the small group lives in a cottage and goes outside to school and to work. Special emphasis on vocational work is given by teaching boys printing, dairying, farming and work in woodshop and shoe-shop. At present there are 396 boys being cared for and with the opening of the two new cottages it will be possible to care for 450 boys.

Samarcand Manor, Samarcand: The act creating this institution for delinquent white girls is somewhat different from that creating the Jackson Training School as it provides that girls may be admitted to the institution by order of court or by voluntary application of the individual, whereas boys are committed to Jackson only by the juvenile court. The law does not set any definite age limit for admission to Samarcand, but due to many urgent cases and the limited accommodations it has been necessary for the board of trustees to make the age limit sixteen in order to care for juvenile delinquents.

This school, established in 1917, is also built on the cottage plan but has never received any aid from the counties. There are five cottages now in use and one in process of construction. The school work ranges from that of the first grade through that of the tenth with special emphasis on vocational education. Classes in home economics, basketry, and millinery alternate with the classes in academic subjects. The girls have opportunity to put these lessons into practice in their cottages. The girls do most of the work on the farm, caring for the cows, pigs and chickens. They have also a garden that supplies the tables in winter as well as in summer. At present there are 210 girls at Samarcand and if the next Legislature makes the appropriation that the board of trustees has asked for, the institution will be able to care for 350 girls.

Morrison Training School for Negro Boys, Hamlet: The General Assembly of 1923 passed a bill authorizing the establishment of an institution for delinquent colored boys. The building has recently been erected and the school will probably open within a short time. It will be supported entirely by the state.

Eastern Carolina Industrial School for Boys, Rocky Mount: This school was authorized at the 1923 session of the Legislature. The buildings were completed in 1925.

Child-Placing: Another important aspect of child welfare work is that of child-placing as opposed to institutional services. Child-placing on a state-wide basis is officially in the hands of the Children's Home Society of North Carolina. This is a private agency, incorporated under the laws of North Carolina, and managed by a board of directors.

Dependent and neglected children in any county in the state are eligible for commitment to this society, through the judge of the juvenile court, if they are normal mentally and physically. At the receiving home in Greensboro the idea is to examine the child physically and mentally; to provide needed treatment and to study the individual child with a view to its placement in a permanent home. The Children's Home Society is doing good work on inadequate funds. It is greatly in need of more field workers for home-finding and supervision. According to the state law the clerk of the court, acting as judge of the juvenile court, has the right to commit children to temporary or permanent homes. Many of the county superintendents of public welfare use this method of child-placing, except in cases where it seems best for the child to remove it entirely from its old environment. Thus, the state is in great need for an agency for child-placing on a temporary basis. The work needs standardizing in the counties— whether this field should be taken over by the State Board of Charities and Public Welfare and a special child-placing agent appointed, or whether the Children's Home Society should increase its activities to take care of this need is a matter for consideration.

Crippled Children: The North Carolina Orthopedic Hospital for Crippled Children at Gastonia is one of the more recent state charitable institutions. It was founded in 1909 by R. B. Babington, made a state institution in 1917, and opened for the admission of patients in July 1921. It has a capacity of sixty beds. Even the first year's operation proved the need of such an institution to be so urgent that the legislature of 1923 increased the previous appropriation. Any child in North Carolina under sixteen who is a cripple can be examined at the State Hospital, and, if found in need of the treatment there provided, can be admitted. At present there is no ward for colored children. This need must soon be met. During the three years since its opening this institution has cared for 1,572 children, according to its annual report. To acquaint the public with the hospital and the nature of its work, a State Census of crippled children was made in October, 1922, in connection with the State Department of Vocational Rehabilitation. Through this census the names of seven hundred children were obtained.

But the problems of distance, poverty and ignorance remained. Local orthopedic clinics were the solution. At present nine of these have been held at which children have been examined; plans for clinics in other counties are in progress. The Surgeon-in-Chief from the hospital and a representative from the Bureau of Child Welfare have been present each time. The clinics have been of great benefit, not only to the children attending them, but to their families as well. Parents have learned that nurses and doctors and social workers are just "folks" to whom they can trust their children—confidence between client and doctor is established—money and time are saved. At the nine clinics held four hundred and sixty-seven names have been added to the original seven hundred. It is hoped that in time these clinics will lead to active efforts to secure a vocational convalescent home school for the children treated at the hospital who need several years' treatment, cases of tubercular joints, etc. During these long periods such patients should have the home and school advantages that they cannot get in their meager private homes.

MENTAL HEALTH AND HYGIENE WORK

The establishment of the Bureau of Mental Health and Hygiene as a department of the State Board of Charities and Public Welfare has marked a definite step in the advancement of the work toward better mental health and hygiene in the State of North Carolina. The Bureau has felt that it must perform a twofold function—the one of an educational, the other of a practical nature. The practical work falls into three divisions: Mental examinations and case investigations, acquisitions and filing data, and inspection of public and private institutions for nervous and mental cases.

The Bureau has sought to bring to the general public the significance of the mentally subnormal and abnormal individuals as community problems by showing their relationship to poverty (eighty-five per cent of the 126 white inmates of eight county homes were either subnormal or abnormal); to delinquency (showing in cases of individual delinquents the importance of the mental condition—the survey of the population of Samarcand Manor); the school problem; and the minor social maladjustments. It has sought, through family history studies, to emphasize the

necessity for preventing the continuation of caco-
genic strains.

That the Bureau has done much of a distinctly
practical nature is evident from the following
summary of the sources from which it has received its cases during the last biennial period:

		No. Cases
I.	Federal Organizations—	
	1. Walter Reed Hospital..................	1
II.	State Departments and Institutions—	
	1. State Board of Charities and Public Welfare 97	
	2. N. C. School for the Deaf........... 268	
	3. Department Vocational Rehabilitation.. 1	
	4. University of North Carolina......... 4	
	5. State Industrial School for Girls...... 233	
	6. N. C. School of Public Welfare, U.N.C. 1	604
III.	County Organizations and Officials—	
	1. Superintendents of Public Welfare.... 53	
	2. School Superintendents.............. 80	
	3. County School Nurses 6	
	4. Court Officials 1	
	5. Health Officers 1	
	6. County Homes..................... 14	155
IV.	Orphanages and Child Placing Societies—	
	1. N. C. Children's Home Society, Greensboro 6	
	2. Oxford Orphanage, Oxford.......... 13	
	3. Thompson Orphanage, Charlotte...... 12	
	4. Wright Refuge, Durham............. 32	63
V.	Miscellaneous—	
	1. Red Cross 2	
	2. Relatives and friends............... 13	

3. Personal application of individual.....   4
4. Attorneys for individual.............   1
5. Secretary of Associated Charities.....   1
6. Woman's Club of Raleigh............   1
7. Church Club of Raleigh.............   1
8. City Commissioners of Asheville......   1   24

PROMOTION AND PUBLICITY WORK

One of the most important tasks of the State
Board of Charities and Public Welfare in which
is needed the coöperation of such groups as the
Federation of Women's Clubs is that of acquainting the people of the state with the plans, programs and purposes of public welfare. With only
seven years since the reorganization of the old
North Carolina Board of Public Charities and the
inauguration of the state-wide county system in
1917, public welfare work in North Carolina is
still comparatively a new venture. Accustomed
for many years to a board of public charities
whose work was more or less desultory and largely
palliative, the people of this state in general have
been ignorant of the aims of the new system,
skeptical of its possibilities and unfamiliar with its
technique. This situation has been steadily improving, however, and with better understanding
of the work, more intelligent people in North
Carolina rally to its support. But there is still
considerable misunderstanding and ignorance of
the real objects of the public welfare work and of
its value.

It is the aim of the publicity bureau of the State Board of Charities and Public Welfare to lessen this misunderstanding and ignorance. In order to be really successful, the State Board of Charities and Public Welfare must "get across" to the people of the state whose board it is, upon whom it depends for support and to whom it is responsible. This is being done by means of news and feature stories on interesting aspects of the work sent out to the state press, by the publication of special bulletins and of "Public Welfare Progress," the Board's monthly sheet, by addresses by the Commissioner of Public Welfare and members of her staff, and by summer institutes of public welfare held at the University of North Carolina for two weeks each year in conjunction with the School of Public Welfare there.

Bulletins: Special bulletins on various phases of the public welfare work are published by the Board when they seem pertinent. Recently bulletins have been issued on Juvenile Courts, Laws Relating to Public Welfare Work in North Carolina, Mothers' Aid, and Poor Relief in North Carolina. A bulletin on child-caring institutions is in process of preparation. These bulletins are furnished. to interested persons upon request.

"Public Welfare Progress": "Public Welfare Progress" is a four-page sheet published monthly by the State Board of Charities and Public Welfare and sent at present to a mailing list of 6,500.

The aim of this publication is to be interesting rather than technical or academic.   It is written for the average reader in order to familiarize him with the work of the Board and to interest him in it.   It is for free distribution.

Addresses: Addresses by the Commissioner of Public Welfare and other members of the staff of the State Board at meetings of organizations of all kinds in the state represent another important part of the publicity carried on in the interest of public welfare work.   It is estimated that during twelve recent months the Commissioner alone has spoken to an average of 1,000 persons a month on the program of public welfare in North Carolina.

Institutes of Public Welfare: For the past five years institutes of public welfare have been held for two weeks each summer at the University of North Carolina under the joint direction of the School of Public Welfare at the University and the State Board of Charities and Public Welfare. At these institutes regular courses of study on subjects relating to public welfare and special lectures by authorities in this field are given.   County superintendents of public welfare and other social workers, public and private, in North Carolina and other parts of the South can gather at these institutes for discussion and study of their particular problems.

Programs for Coöperating Organizations: Suggestive programs in line with the State program of public welfare are prepared by the publicity bureau for organizations wishing to cooperate with the State Board of Charities and Public Welfare.

News and Feature Stories to the State Press: News stories about the work of the State Board of Charities and Public Welfare and feature stories about aspects of the public welfare work that seem to call for special attention are prepared by the publicity bureau and sent to the newspapers of the state.

The Four-County Demonstration of Public Welfare: In the effort to demonstrate to North Carolina and to many others interested, a plan has been evolved by the State Board of Charities and Public Welfare and the School of Public Welfare of the University of North Carolina whereby a four-county demonstration covering a period of three years is being undertaken to show what can be done in two rural and two urban communities. The plan will provide that the State Board of Charities and Public Welfare and the School of Public Welfare furnish adequate assistance to these counties to make possible a minimum organization, some of the details of which the counties may not deem necessary. Such a plan includes an expert case-work supervisor, more assistants in psychiatric social work, assistants in probation and school-attendance work, a colored assistant to help work out problems among the negroes, together with other necessary material and equipment. The result of the work ought to show the point at which counties may extend their services to the best advantage and the minimum below which they cannot go in order to reap benefits from the county-unit system and state coöperation. This demonstration has been made possible by the coöperation of the Laura Spelman Rockefeller Memorial which is interested, along with the rest of us, in helping determine the relative merits of the North Carolina county plan.

Special Plans and Projects: In addition to the attempts at promotion and publicity on the part of the State Department, the counties themselves have entered upon special plans and projects. In one county, the women who are recipients of Mothers' Aid have been organized in a club which meets once a month, and which is both recreational and educational in purpose. Mental hygiene clinics are held in some of the counties; temporary homes for dependent, neglected and delinquent children have been established; emergency relief funds have been set aside in some counties by public-spirited citizens. These are only a few things being done by the different counties.

RECURRING PROBLEMS AND RECOMMENDATIONS

So far, attention has been directed mainly toward the constructive work of the public welfare system without any special reference to particular problems and difficulties, except as involved in the work of the several bureaus.

Trained Workers: One of the greatest difficulties in the way of effective work is the lack of trained workers who can see through the administration of the North Carolina plan and the wishes of the forward-looking counties. This is not different from the problem which faced the county superintendents of schools a few decades ago or the problem which faced the teachers and the educational system before higher standards and certification were introduced. It is, nevertheless, a very vital problem and one that must be worked out before progress can be made satisfactorily. Almost simultaneously with the establishment of the new plan of public welfare in North Carolina, the University established a School of Public Welfare with this particular problem in view. One of the forms of coöperation between the School of Public Welfare and the State Board of Charities and Public Welfare is that found in the institutes previously described. One objective of the four-county demonstration above mentioned is to insure better field work and a social laboratory for the students in training at the University. The School of Public Welfare also stands ready to coöperate with the State Board of Charities and Public Welfare whenever it can render service in study, research, or coöperative venture. The beginning of the fourth year of the school finds a very substantial group of students and the effectiveness of instruction and field work is greatly accentuated by the coöperation of members of the staff of the State Board of Charities and of Public Welfare. Another important coöperative act has been the scholarship granted by the State Federation of Women's Clubs awarded each year to a North Carolina young woman preparing for professional social work.

Coöperation with Other Agencies: Development of the program of public welfare in North Carolina can be greatly increased by coöperation between the state agencies and civic and benevolent organizations, state or local. Such organizations as the North Carolina Federation of Women's Clubs and local Women's Clubs, the North Carolina League of Women Voters, the North Carolina Federation of Business and Professional Women's Clubs and the North Carolina Legislative Council of Women have shown hearty interest in the public welfare work and the desire to align their social service programs with the state program of public welfare. Also churches, missionary societies, and women's auxiliaries are manifesting a growing interest in public welfare. Other civic and benevolent associations such as the Rotary, Kiwanis, Civitan and Lion's Clubs, the Masons, the Odd Fellows, the Red Men, Knights of Pythias, Junior Order, B. P. O. E., have given valuable coöperation to the public wel-

fare work, notably in helping to secure the passage
of the Mothers' Aid law and in the work for
crippled children.

County Boards of Public Welfare: The powers
of county boards of public welfare should be enlarged so that their members may have some voice
in the appointment of the county superintendent
of public welfare who, under the present law, is
chosen by the county commissioners and the
county board of education. The county board of
public welfare now serves only in an advisory capacity to the county superintendent of public welfare, and its responsibility is so slight that, except
in the case of members especially interested in the
work, the board is apt to be less effective than it
should be. The idea that service on the county
board of public welfare is valuable public service
should be encouraged.

Prison Conditions: There should be a continuing board of directors for the State Prison. This
is necessary for an unbroken and constructive
policy of prison administration. As constituted
at the present, the entire personnel of the board of
directors of the State Prison may be changed
every four years. The State Board of Health, the
State Board of Agriculture, the State Board of
Charities and Public Welfare and the board of
every other state institution is a continuing board.
What has been found to be a satisfactory policy

for the organization of these boards should apply equally to the State Prison.

A separate prison for women under a separate board is needed. Separation of men and women in penal institutions is essential in the conduct of a good system. There are any number of women offenders in North Carolina who need corrective punishment and physical treatment for whom the state is now doing practically nothing on account of inadequate institutional facilities.

A study of the county chain-gang system should be made. This system should be studied both as an economic and as a social problem with the idea of transferring control of these prisoners to the state.

Women in Charge of Women Prisoners: Whole-time or part-time matrons should be employed in all jails in which women prisoners are confined. These matrons should carry the keys to the cells of the women prisoners which are now generally carried by men, the jailers. Furthermore, women should accompany delinquents and feeble-minded girls or women to State institutions.

A Whole-Time Superintendent of Public Welfare in Every County: and in the Larger Counties Additional Officers to Assist Him: The public welfare system in North Carolina can never hope for full success until every county is organized for the work with a whole-time superintendent of public welfare. No part-time officer can fulfill all the duties of the position which, as a matter of fact, are too great for any one person. And it cannot be expected that the superintendent of schools who acts as ex-officio welfare officer in counties where there is none can discharge these duties in addition to his regular work. Every county in the state has its unfortunate people, the delinquent, the dependent, the defective and the neglected, who should be under the supervision of an officer directly responsible for their care, as the superintendent of public welfare is. In the larger counties the superintendent of public welfare should have adequate assistance by probation officers and school attendance officer, and clerical help.

A Better Understanding of Public Welfare: But after all perhaps the greatest problem in North Carolina is still one of interpreting the meaning of public welfare to all the people. This applies scarcely less to the highest officials, to the college professor and professional man, than to the great mass of people throughout the state. It does not help matters to say that such a condition exists in other states also. What is needed is to get out of people's minds the twofold impression that public welfare is, on the one hand merely a sentimental, supplemental sort of work, and on the other the impression that it has always been and therefore must always be subject to careless methods and political influence. This is, of course, a difficult problem and one which will take a great deal of time. It will involve the doing of good work by the State Board of Charities and Public Welfare and by the county systems. It will involve the other problems already mentioned. It seems but fair to say that North Carolina has made some progress in this direction and that the system as a whole has been successful, as may clearly be seen from the story which has just been presented in this chapter.

CHAPTER X

THE COUNTY AS A UNIT FOR PUBLIC WELFARE

RECENT EMERGENCE OF THE RURAL PROBLEM

AMERICAN programs of social service are urban born. Hebrew tradition has it that the first city was built by the first murderer, and throughout history cities have had an unenviable reputation as destroyers of populations, as social vortices forever dragging down the race to physical and spiritual ruin. It is not strange that we should have discovered our social problems where tradition had convinced us we should find them, and that in consequence American social work should attain its primary growth in an urban environment. It was in the city that we first became aware of such problems as health, destitution, crime, unemployment, family disintegration, recreation, etc., and our social service programs have come to have a predominantly urban cast. Hence until recent years the major portion of social effort has been exerted on behalf of a minority of the population. "Man made the city, God made the country," we naively said, and left it largely to the Almighty to keep watch above His own. But recently have we become aware of what a multitude of rural conditions there are with the initiation and perpetuation of which the Almighty has probably had very little to do. Pure milk, pure minds and pure morals are not the omnipresent rural trinity we had supposed. We have discovered the rural communities as "the unequal places of American democracy," and out of the discovery there has emerged within the past decade a new problem: How shall we make available in these unequal places the technique and standards of service which have been developed in urban communities?

EARLY VOLUNTARY AGENCIES AND THE COUNTY UNIT

The New York State Charities Aid Association. While this problem has been in process of formulation, experiments have been going forward along many lines which furnish us the data for its solution. One of the earliest of these experiments was that of the New York Charities Aid Association. The inadequacy of the state's institutional care of the destitute and the ill led a group of public-spirited citizens to organize a society to study the needs of these classes, and to aid in improving the methods employed by tax-supported charities in caring for these wards of the state. This was in 1872. Because of the importance of the county in the administration of public charities, the State Charities Aid Association adopted at the outset the county plan of organization. In addition to the central association with headquarters in New York City, county committees were formed, each studying the problems of its county, and all coördinated by the central association in working on behalf of state-wide programs of public welfare. The original plan contemplated a program of service for three groups, (1) dependent children, (2) adult paupers and (3) inmates of hospitals. In the earlier stages of the work, however, activities on behalf of the first group overshadowed all the others. A law was secured prohibiting the commitment of destitute children to almshouses, and making the overseers of the poor responsible for their maintenance in "appropriate institutions for the support and care of children." As the children were removed from the almshouses the newly organized county committees became active in aiding the poor-law officials in caring for their wards in foster homes. Later temporary boarding homes were added, and finally, in 1898 the central association organized a placing out agency to unify and standardize the work of the county committees throughout the state. As a concrete example of the method employed by the county committees in improving the tax-supported welfare work we may cite the Newburgh Plan. In 1877 Newburgh had built a children's home which in 1894 the commissioners of charities proposed to enlarge. But the Newburgh Committee of the State Charities Aid Association secured postponement of action until the situation could be thoroughly studied. The outcome of their investigation showed that some of the children now in the institution could be returned to their homes, others could be placed in free foster homes, and still others could be transferred to the State Home for Feebleminded Children. Thus the population of the institution was so reduced that no enlargement was required. But the results of the investigation were more far reaching. Child-placing in the county had been inadequately supervised, and visitation disclosed children previously placed in foster homes as living in unfavorable environments. The family circumstances of children for whom public support was asked were investigated. Frequently hidden resources were discovered and care provided which prevented family disintegration and saved public funds. Finally, after a period of demonstration at the expense of the private agency, a plan was drawn up providing for the joint maintenance of the work by private and public funds. Thus originated the Newburgh Plan, which has now been extended to more than a score of counties of the Empire State.

The work of the State Charities Aid Association has by no means been confined to the child welfare field. Ever since its inception this organization has been creating public opinion with reference to more adequate standards of public service on behalf of disadvantaged groups, and has been conducting experiments in coöperation with tax-supported agencies through which the opinion created might be made practically effective. As in the case of child welfare, most of these experiments took the form of county unit programs, owing to the significance of the county traditionally as an administrative unit in the public welfare program of the state.

Child Welfare Work in Other States. As in New York, so also in other states, it is child welfare work that has led the way in the reorganization of public welfare activities on a county basis, until in many of the states, either through public or private agencies or through a combination of both, there exist facilities through which there can be made available on behalf of the dependent, delinquent or neglected child in the remotest rural township the same technique of investigation and standards of treatment which were once confined to urban groups.

The Iowa Plan. Another series of experiments in county organization has been carried out in Iowa, beginning at Grinnell in 1912. The Iowa Plan in its most representative form contemplates the formation of a central social service bureau or league composed of representative citizens, with the members of the county board of supervisors acting as members ex officio. In this board are centered the private social agencies of the county. It also administers the county outdoor relief. This

is secured by having the secretary of the social
service league appointed overseer of the poor.
Such appointment is of course purely voluntary on
the part of the county board of supervisors. It
has been adopted in a number of counties, though
in some of these the services rendered have been
centered in certain communities or townships
rather than covering the county as a whole.

*The Monmouth County Organization for Social
Service.* In the meantime similar developments
have been taking place in other states. In New
Jersey the Monmouth County Branch of the New
Jersey State Charities Aid and Prison Reform
Association has since 1912 been coördinating the
activities of the major public welfare agencies of
the county and developing a program of case work
reaching those areas of the county not now cov-
ered by other case-working agencies. This agency
has also demonstrated the value of county organization in coördinating the activities of local and
state-wide agencies.

"It is understood at the state department that
the county organization is to be notified at once of
every admission from the county to a state institution, and of the anticipated parole from an institution of every Monmouth county ward. The organization assumes responsibility for investigating the circumstances of commitment and secures
a history of the subject. If family problems are
involved, it begins to work upon them, so that the

improvement in conditions may be coincident with the improvement in the individual under state care, if that is possible. The organization also receives the report of state examiners concerning the subject under care. These reports often throw light on the family problem, just as the facts of family and personal history, gleaned by the county, assist the state agent to understand the patient. When a ward of the state received from this county is released, the county organization takes up the burden of placement and supervision, coördinating its plans with those of the parole bureau of the state department under whose authority the subject remains until the expiration of the parole period."[1]

The foregoing citations of experience in this field are representative, not inclusive. It will be noted, however, that they represent on the one hand either the unofficial attempts of private organizations to coöperate with and so raise the standards of public welfare agencies, as in the case of the New Jersey, New York and Iowa experiments, or, on the other, the official attempts to place the work of tax-supported agencies on a more adequate technical basis by confining attention to specialized fields, as in the case of the child welfare programs of various states. In other words, where the work has been more or less in-

[1] County Organization and Child Care. U. S. Dept. of Labor. Children's Bureau Bulletin No. 107, p. 90.

tensive in scope of service it has been organized on a voluntary basis, and where it has been organized as an official state function it has been narrowed in scope to a specialized class of clients.

MUNICIPAL DEPARTMENTS OF PUBLIC WELFARE

The first attempts at comprehensive reorganization of public welfare administration took place in certain cities of the Middle West. In April, 1910, the first Board of Public Welfare in the United States was organized at Kansas City. It was the outgrowth of the appreciation on the part of the Kansas City Board of Pardons and Paroles of the need of supervision of the conditions affecting the discharged prisoner. The board from the first exercised inclusive functions. It assumed the full burden of the city's responsibility toward the poor, the delinquent, the unemployed, the deserted and the otherwise unfortunate. It undertook the endorsement of private agencies, the operation of a confidential exchange, a legal aid bureau, an employment bureau, the licensing of dance halls, the supervision of commercialized amusements, including the censorship of motion pictures. It promoted factory inspection, sanitation and safety. It operated a municipal quarry in which any able-bodied man could earn meals for himself or groceries and coal for his family. It conducted a child welfare exhibit. It undertook social research into such community problems as private charities, housing, recreation, conditions affecting working women, the social evil, desertion and non-support, cost of workingmen's houses, drug addiction, child labor, crippled children, etc. This form of organization has spread rapidly. Although but thirteen years have passed since its first appearance, it has been adopted by nearly half a hundred cities containing a third of the population of the United States.

COUNTY DEPARTMENTS OF PUBLIC WELFARE

Shortly after the organization of the Kansas City Board its general superintendent, Mr. L. A. Halbert, outlined before a public meeting in Topeka, Kansas, a plan whereby the Kansas City system might be adapted to the smaller communities of Kansas. The outcome of Mr. Halbert's work in this field was a plan making the county the administrative unit in public welfare work, and providing the appointment of county superintendents of public welfare. As Mr. Halbert describes it, "The plan calls for the consolidation of all the social work to be done by the county into one department with a skilled superintendent and a staff as needed. The contemplated activities include outdoor relief, parole and probations work for adults and juveniles of the county—whether released from the local courts or from state institutions—after-care of the insane, employment finding, child-placing, truancy work, censorship of commercial recreation, public health work, etc. In counties with no great cities, these things are usually either neglected or made incidental duties of officers whose main interests lie in other directions. They can never be skillfully done so long as they are organized in that way.

"This plan unifies and systematizes the social betterment work of each county and concentrates it under one board. It provides a local agency that comes in close personal touch with the unfortunate and their problems in a way formerly only reached by a state agency at a great distance.

"Combining all the various kinds of social work makes it possible to have at least one skilled social worker in every county, whereas it is not practical to have in every county a juvenile probation officer, an adult probation officer, a poor commissioner to administer outdoor relief, an agent of the free employment bureaus, an agent for placing dependent children in foster homes, an inspector of commercial amusements, etc. But it is practical to combine all these functions in one good, high-class, all-round social worker, even in small counties, and in larger counties it is possible to have the force of workers adapted exactly to the needs of the county."[2]

Special County Boards of Public Welfare. The first piece of social legislation providing for a

---

[2] Halbert, L. A. Boards of Public Welfare. Proceedings National Conference of Social Work. 1918, p. 224.

County Board of Public Welfare seems to have been that of Missouri, under which, in January, 1913, St. Joseph secured a combination city and county board. The Cook County, Illinois, department of public welfare soon followed, but its scope was limited to the handling of relief cases. In California the large measure of home rule granted to counties, together with a statute permitting county boards of supervisors to delegate the investigation and periodic visitation of all persons receiving relief, enabled the city and county of Los Angeles to establish in 1914 a public welfare department with broad administrative powers. Since then, under the leadership of the State Board, the plan has been enlarged in scope and extended to other counties, until at present twelve out of the fifty-eight counties of the state,[3] containing thirty per cent of the population, have bodies variously known as departments of public welfare, welfare councils, welfare commissions, and social service commissions.

In 1916 the New York legislature, by a piece of special legislation applying only to Westchester county, created the office of county commissioner of public welfare. The commissioner of public welfare is one of the higher-salaried county officials, and is elected for a term of three years. The work is organized in six departments: the alms-

---

[3] County Organization and Child Care. U. S. Dept. of Labor. Children's Bureau Bulletin No. 107, p. 56.

house department, the department of hospitals and health, of corrections, the farm department, the purchasing department and the department of child welfare. Each department is presided over by a specialist in his field appointed by the commissioner and responsible to him. Thus there has been recognized and enacted into law a principle of administration which permits of gradual extension throughout the state, and there is becoming available a fund of experience as an aid in promoting and directing the process.

The North Carolina State-wide Plan.[4] Since 1916 events have moved rapidly. As yet the attempts at administrative reorganization of public welfare work, whether voluntary or official, have been confined to urban communities, or to counties with a large urban nucleus. Up until 1917 no direct attack on a large scale had been made upon the problem formulated above. How shall we make available to every rural community of the state the technique and standards of service now attainable in urban centers? During this year, however, North Carolina initiated such a state-wide attack, in the law creating the State Board of Charities and Public Welfare and making provision for the county system of organization. The legislation was strengthened in 1919, and the effective development of the system dates from that year. The State Board is composed of seven un-

---

[4] For a fuller description of the North Carolina plan see Chap. IX.

paid members appointed by the governor. This Board selects the State Commissioner of Public Welfare and appoints in each of the counties an advisory board of three, known as the County Board of Charities and Public Welfare. This appointment is mandatory. Another mandatory feature of the law is the appointment by the board of county commissioners and the county board of education sitting jointly of a County Superintendent of Public Welfare, whose appointment must in turn be approved by the State Commissioner. Counties of 32,000 population and over must have a full-time superintendent. In counties of less population the duties of the county superintendent of public welfare may be assigned to the county superintendent of schools, who receives no extra salary for the work, but who may be provided with the necessary assistance in performing these additional duties.

The powers of the county superintendent of public welfare under the law are such that if he carries them out as prescribed by the law he will of necessity work in coöperation with all the organized philanthropic, political, judicial, religious and educational organizations at work in the county whether under public or private auspices, and make of his office a coördinating and standardizing agency of vast significance. Such is in fact the tendency in practice.

The Missouri Plan. In 1921 the Missouri legislature passed a law in many respects similar to that of North Carolina. There are, however, important differences in organization. The North Carolina system is more highly centralized than that of Missouri. Thus, the Missouri law is permissive, not mandatory, and the appointment of the county superintendent is vested in the county courts, with no veto lodged in the state board. The duties of the county superintendent in Missouri are:

"A. Constructive relief of poverty.

"B. Proper care and placing of homeless, orphaned and neglected children.

"C. Effective enumeration, education and physical treatment of every handicapped child, including deaf, blind, crippled and feebleminded.

"D. Modern treatment of delinquency.

"E. Strict enforcement of child labor and school attendance laws.

"F. Intelligent care of mental defectives.

"G. Promotion of wholesome recreation and the elimination of undesirable influences in public amusements.

"H. Organization of community resources for public health improvements, etc.

"I. Studying causes of social problems and instituting programs of education and prevention."[5]

---

[5] Kuhlman, A. F. Development of County Public Welfare Work in Missouri. Annals American Academy of Political and Social Science, Jan. 1923, p. 131f.

At the beginning of this year thirteen counties of the state had put the plan into effect, and had superintendents of public welfare actually in service. In addition there were a number of counties having the appointment of superintendents under serious consideration.

ADVANTAGES OF THE COUNTY UNIT

Certain advantages of the county plan of public welfare work have been implied throughout this discussion. First, it utilizes as a unit of administration the county, the one nation-wide unit of local self government in America. The township is only a local peculiarity of a minority of the states of the American commonwealth. In twenty-six states it does not exist at all; in five additional states it exists in name only; in but seventeen states does it play any vital role as a unit of local government.[6] The municipalities, on the other hand, though they now contain a majority of the American people, cover but an infinitesimally small percentage of our territory. But the county is all pervasive. It, or its equivalent, the parish, exists in all the states. It is the only unit of local self-government with which a considerable proportion of the American people have any direct and personal experience. It is startling that it should have been until recently so largely ignored by political scientists and that it should so long

[6] Porter, Kirk H. County and Township Government in the United States, p. 308.

have remained our political blind spot in civic education. Voluminous texts and hours of class-room discussion are devoted to the functions of municipal, state and national government, while the most significant unit of local government has been practically ignored in both the literature and the teaching of civics. Yet the laboratory of good citizenship is not so much the nation at large, where forces are complex and the processes whereby public opinion secures concrete expression in policy are slow and devious, but in the counties, where the citizen is in direct contact with a multiplicity of controllable conditions, and where the methods of control are direct and effective.

Again, the county has advantages in area and population. The state is too large, the local community too small. With modern methods of communication and transportation the workers can know intimately and visit frequently and expeditiously the entire area they serve. The population, outside of urban counties, is small enough to permit of effective organization and a correlated program covering a wide range of services. It is large enough, outside of frontier communities, to permit of adequate financing with no appreciable difference in the tax levy. Indeed, in many instances the county unit has financed itself through savings in outdoor poor relief and reducing the number of county wards through uncovering hidden resources.

Third, many private agencies, whose work must of necessity be correlated with the new county plan of public welfare, have developed county programs in the rural field. Thus, the Y. M. C. A. through a process of experimentation, has found the county to be the best unit of rural administration. Following the lead of the older organization, the Y. W. C. A. has organized its Town and County Department on a county basis. Recent years have witnessed the extension of such movements as charity organization, public health nursing, anti-tuberculosis propaganda, etc., to rural areas with the county as the unit of service and education. The work of these agencies, together with that of the Farm Bureaus, county agricultural and home demonstration agents, and the boys' and girls' club work of the States Relations Service of the United States Department of Agriculture, has reacted upon the units of county government and stimulated them to greater activity in the field of rural welfare. No national agency has exercised a wider or more profound influence in this field than the American Red Cross. The assistance given by local chapters to soldiers' families during the war involved rural and small-town families and demonstrated to thousands of rural communities their need of organized social work. With demobilization, under the happy title of Home Service this family welfare work was extended to civilian families in territory where there was no other organization in the field. This meant practically the whole of rural United States. The work is in charge of a county secretary, supported by a local Home Service Committee in as many communities as can be sufficiently interested. This committee advises with and assists the county worker in carrying out the local program.

There are, however, certain more specific advantages in the county plan of administration through a superintendent of public welfare which we have not heretofore implied. First of all, it is a means through which we may more adequately recognize the nature of rural social work. It is not material relief, it is not conventional case work for the socially inadequate that our rural society most needs, but that trained and capable leadership which shall enable the rural community to achieve for itself a richer and a fuller life. Community organization, community planning, the widening of the horizon of rural life through social education, its reorganization so as to provide adequate leisure and the provision of social means and institutions for the profitable utilization of the leisure available or anticipated—these are some of the social projects which we must carry out if we are to prevent the decay of rural institutions which our rural surveys have so strikingly revealed, and to reverse the process of rural "folk depletion" of which Professor Ross has so effectively written.[7]

---

[7] Ross, E. A. The Social Trend.

An analysis of the situation in Indiana reveals in a striking way the extent and urgent character of this problem of rural reconstruction in that state. Although her population increased 8.5 per cent between 1910 and 1920, this increase was largely confined to a few urban centers. Sixty-four, or 69.6 per cent, of her ninety-two counties lost population. Of the twenty-eight counties which show an increase, in eight the increase was negligible, in nine it ranged from five to fifteen per cent, in seven from five to twenty-five, in three from twenty-five to fifty per cent, in one, Lake, the increase was ninety-three per cent. In only twenty counties was there an appreciable increase.[8]

If we confine our attention to the rural areas the situation is still more striking. Twenty-two of the counties are classified by the census as strictly rural, that is, they contain no municipality of 2,500 inhabitants or more.[9] These twenty-two counties had in 1900 a population of 318,928. By 1910 it had declined to 301,898, or 5.3 per cent, and by 1920 to 281,641, or 6.7 per cent. Since the dawn of this century these twenty-two counties have lost 37,287 or 11.7 of their population. In sixty-one additional counties the rural population

---

[8] XIV Census, Vol. I, p. 102f.

[9] These counties are Benton, Brown, Carroll, Crawford, Franklin, Harrison, Hendricks, La Grange, Martin, Newton, Ohio, Orange, Parke, Pike, Pulaski, Ripley, Scott, Starke, Switzerland, Union, and Warren.

has declined since 1910.   In only nine counties did
the rural population increase.[10]   In three of these
the increase was negligible; in only six was it significant, and in these six the increase was largely
in the hamlets and unincorporated villages rather
than in the open country.   In spite of an 8.5 per
cent increase in population for the state as a
whole, rural Indiana lost 109,506 or 7 per cent
from 1910 to 1920, and an additional 96,732 or
5.8 per cent in the preceding decade.   In other
words, there are now living in rural Indiana 206,-
235 or 12.5% fewer people than at the beginning
of the century.   Greater than the total American
world war losses, greater than the losses on both
sides in the four years of the Civil War, has been
the loss to the rural population of this state in
twenty years.   Can a rural society lose a quarter
of a million people in less than a quarter of a century and not give rise to grave problems of community organization and leadership which social
work of the traditional type scarcely touches?
Such are the data with which the county unit plan
seeks an accounting.

Another advantage of the county unit plan is
that it recognizes the significance of personal contacts in promoting newer ideals of public welfare.
Social work may well profit by the experience of
scientific agriculture.   The literature prepared by

---

[10] XIV Census, Vol. I, p. 156.

the government's experts accumulated dust at Washington, or was franked by congressmen to their rural constituents, who used it to start the kitchen fire. Only through personal contacts, through the exhibit cars, the local demonstration plots and the county agent has the movement made headway. Similarly, we cannot promote effective case work by correspondence, or group work by radio. Only by local demonstration in the counties can we create a public opinion extensive enough in scope and intelligent enough in character to sustain an adequate state-wide social service program. Social legislation lags or remains a dead letter upon the state books so far as a multitude of communities are concerned because there is no trained person in the locality interested in making it understood or responsible for making it effective. Such an educator and interpreter the county unit plan provides.

The plan possesses the additional advantage of plasticity. In the smaller counties and in the more sparsely settled regions the same superintendent may serve adjoining counties on a part-time basis until the development of the program or the increase of the available resources makes more extensive work possible. On the other hand, in the larger counties there is the possibility, under a common superintendency, of whatever departmentalizing, specializing or districting the situation calls for. It is also plastic as to functions.

These can be made as inclusive as local conditions require. Certainly the general tasks of promotion and coördination will be included, but other detailed functions, such as public health, may well vary between states or between counties within the same state. Detailed uniformity stifles local effectiveness.

How shall the county welfare program be correlated with the programs of the private agencies, some of them county-wide, others more restricted in area served? The experience of Pennsylvania is of interest here. Pennsylvania lacks the county unit plan, the four bureaus of the State Department of Public Welfare working directly in the counties through their staff representatives. In order, however, to avoid confusion of purpose and waste of effort, the state department has undertaken the promotion of County Councils of Social Agencies. These bring together all private social agencies working in the county and make possible the coördination of all voluntary effort on behalf of the social welfare. Five representatives from this county council of social agencies are then chosen, who with five county officials, constitute the County Board of Public Welfare. These five officials include the County Superintendent of Schools, the County Medical Director, and one representative each from the County Commissioners and the Directors of the Poor. The Board is completed by the appointment by central state authority of an eleventh member who acts as chairman. The functions of the County Boards of Public Welfare are "to harmonize the activities of official and unofficial agencies, to keep the state departments informed as to the needs in the county, and to carry over into local districts the best methods of work of general public welfare."[11]

A county board of public welfare thus constituted could be made an effective instrument of correlation between public and private agencies if incorporated into the North Carolina or the Missouri plan of superintendency, with such modifications as would be necessitated by differences in the organization of the central state authority.

Many controversial questions are here purposely avoided. How shall the system be inaugurated in the counties when once adopted by legislative action? Shall it be mandatory upon the counties, as in North Carolina, or permissive, as in Missouri? How shall the county superintendent be appointed to give assurance of adequate training and experience? How comprehensive shall be his functions and powers? How would the county plan need to be modified for any specific state in view of its specific needs? These, and other details of policy, must be worked out for each state on the

---

[11] Hunt, C. V. The Department of Public Welfare in Pennsylvania. Annals American Academy of Political and Social Science, Jan. 1923. p. 112.

basis of local requirements. The scope of the present discussion has therefore been limited to pointing out the needs and the possibilities of organization for more effective social work in the rural counties, and to summarizing American experience in this field of administration.

CHAPTER XI

THE CITY PLAN OF PUBLIC WELFARE
ADMINISTRATION

MUNICIPAL survey and investigations made in recent years have brought out conclusively the fact that, no matter how tardy or advanced the public welfare *administration* carried on by large American cities may be, their *problems and needs* (as summarized elsewhere in this article) are about the same. To be sure, there are cities below the 200,000 population level presenting similar problems but there are others also, in which the situation is much simpler. Above the 750,000 population level are the four cities of New York, Chicago, Philadelphia, and Detroit; but their public welfare problems, though likewise similar, are more complex and specialized and merit separate treatment. The present article, therefore, deals only with public welfare administration in the thirty cities in question.

The object of the article is to submit a plan for the organization of a modern Department of Public Welfare in cities of the size indicated, together with the functions and purposes of such a department, as seen in the experience of cities that have already established the same, and the advantages and economies that may reasonably be expected to result.

PUBLIC AND PRIVATE WELFARE ACTIVITIES

Since cities differ considerably as to the stage of public welfare administration reached, it might seem offhand that a plan of departmental organization devised for one city could hardly be applied to another. The sequel will show that in this respect the stage of administrative development reached in a city, prior to the establishment of a Department of Public Welfare, is of small consequence. A composite of existing conditions might be assumed, but for the sake of concreteness, (and since it answers the same purpose) the writer has indicated below the public welfare activities actually carried on by a city chosen at random from the group herein considered, and will endeavor to show how such activities can be organized into a modern Department of Public Welfare. In the end it will be obvious that public welfare activities can be substituted for, deducted from or added to this list without changing the organization plan.

The city the writer has in mind administers the following public welfare activities, excluding the activities of the Department of Health, which logically stands by itself:

(a) Department of the Overseer of the Poor— taking care of applications for outdoor relief and prosecuting bastardy and non-support cases;

(b) Almshouse for the aged and infirm poor who have become public charges;

(c) Municipal Employment Bureau, serving especially the needs of the other public welfare bureaus but taking on extraordinary duties during unemployment crises;

(d) Home for Delinquent Children;

(e) Summer camp for the worthy poor;

(f) Public bath houses;

(g) Band concerts.

In the city there are, also, many private relief and benevolent societies and associations, among which are included the following groups:

(a) Bureau of Associated Charities, comprehending a number of specialized agencies for helping needy families; fraternal, religious and mutual benefit societies; free loan, legal aid, burial, fresh air outing, day nursery and other societies rendering special aid to the needy;

(b) Private homes for the aged and infirm— for catholics, protestants, racial groups, and other special groups;

(c) Societies concerned mainly with the unemployed and the homeless, providing work, lodgings, food, transportation;

(d) Agencies for the prevention of cruelty to children, adoption societies, private orphan asylums, child labor and welfare associations, and homes for incorrigible and delinquent children;

(e) Special reform agencies for wayward girls, inebriates, mendicants, and the like;

(f) Agencies and schools for the epileptic, insane, crippled, deaf, blind, and other specially handicapped groups;

(g) Associations to provide recreation, playgrounds, social centers, thrift and savings facilities, and so on.

It cannot be assumed that every city of from a quarter to three-quarters of a million population has developed all of these specialized private welfare agencies, which have nevertheless become legion in the past decade. Some cities have developed them more in one direction, others in another; and the public welfare administration of a city has often filled in the gaps. Furthermore, these private welfare agencies have developed so rapidly in recent years that much duplication of effort, both as between the agencies themselves and between them and city departments, has resulted. In addition, numerous fraudulent schemes are continually being launched and these bid for support along with the worthy agencies, so that all in all it has become imperative to organize the private field to weed out unworthy activities and eliminate duplication as between worthy charities.

In organizing the field of private philanthropy in large cities the following four developments have been outstanding:

(a) A general federation of private welfare, relief and benevolent societies;

(b) A confidential exchange of information concerning families and individuals which the various private agencies are aiding;

(c) A method of endorsement to cover worthy private charities;

(d) A common budget to cover the financial needs of endorsed private charities.

It is not the purpose of this article to go into detail regarding developments in the private welfare field, but, here again, it cannot be assumed that all large cities have gone all the way or even very far in these matters or, where they have, that these centralizing and coördinating mechanisms of private philanthropy have always been worked out effectively. Where they have worked poorly, the organization of a modern Department of Public Welfare in the city has often aided materially in rendering these mechanisms effective and the department has even operated some of them until organized private philanthropy could be strengthened to take them over. In fact, it is held by some authorities that it is the city's duty to prevent unworthy charities from operating, and license and inspection powers have sometimes been evoked for the purpose. At any rate, it is very important that the city Department of Public Welfare have a strong and trustworthy Confidential Exchange and General Federation to work with. Even though waste and duplication of effort were eliminated as between the private agencies themselves (a consummation devoutly to be wished but as yet not very much in evidence), there is still the task of even greater importance, as far as it concerns the city itself, and that is the task of eliminating duplication of effort between the welfare activities administered by the city and those carried on by private philanthropy. The unprecedented development of specialized private agencies in recent years has made this problem a most urgent one for every large city.

NEED FOR PUBLIC WELFARE CLEARING HOUSE

To meet this problem of duplication of effort between public and private welfare activities, it is necessary to establish a public welfare clearing house. A brief review of a city's public welfare activities in the light of modern development makes this clearly evident.

The department of the overseer of the poor as usually operated has its roots in legislation enacted many years ago. It concerns itself primarily with *material* relief, whereas constructive *rehabilitation* has become a modern criterion. It is forced by its traditions and legal limitations to deal mainly with *individuals* whereas modern welfare recognizes the *family* as the center of the relief problem. As a result, private welfare agencies almost invariably do what constructive work is carried on while the city hands out doles, too often unnecessarily. Furthermore, in giving material aid the city is frequently duplicating precisely what some private agency is doing.

An examination of causal factors leading to destitution and dependency will serve to illustrate. Among the most important of these causal factors are sickness, unemployment, intemperance, accident, immorality, mental derangement, blindness, desertion, old age. A needy case coming before the overseer because of sickness, should be handled also by the medical director, possibly also by the tuberculosis association, shut-in society, or nursing association; unemployment involves the municipal employment bureau and possibly also church relief, or the free-loan society; intemperance may require institutional care at a home for inebriates or prosecution for non-support; accident cases may come under a workmen's compensation law; immorality may need the aid of the courts or a Florence Crittenton League and a child-placing agency; blindness or other disability has its special private agencies to cope with it; old age involves many private agencies as well as the city almshouse; and in cases where material aid is imperative, there are private charities, day nurseries, loan associations, legal aid and advice which might be called in to help. From these illustrations it is readily seen that material relief may or may not be important or necessary in any given case and that a proper study of family relationships and causal factors not apparent on the surface often obviates the necessity of the overseer of the poor extending any material aid at all.

The overseer of the poor does not and cannot make anything but a cursory investigation into cases of need, nor is he in a position to know intimately the scores of specialized private agencies that might be of assistance in each particular instance. As far as he is concerned, alleged material need forces him to act, and unless there is some centralized public welfare clearing house, through which the coöperation of all agencies logically involved is secured, there is no assurance that duplication of effort will not occur or that constructive help will be rendered.

Similar illustrations might be drawn from other public welfare activities carried on by the large city. With respect to almshouses, it is often said that they do not keep adequate records, do not make full investigation of cases entering, do not secure the help they might secure from outside agencies (such as furnishing entertainments or securing gifts of flowers or magazines), and that they do not pretend to rehabilitate those of the infirm that might be rehabilitated. Here, again, the superintendent of the almshouse cannot attend to these wider aspects of welfare. These can only be taken care of by a fuller bringing together of other welfare interests through a municipal clearing house organized for the purpose. Likewise the work of the municipal employment bureau, home for delinquent children (especially in its parole and follow-up work), various public recreational ventures such as summer camps, public baths, band concerts, and other public welfare activities—all need coördination and proper dovetailing with the work of private agencies to render their service to the community economical and efficient.

In brief, the fact that in the modern large American city there are operative many specialized private welfare agencies, some attempting to do precisely what the city is doing, some overlapping here and there, others logically supplementing the city's work but unable to do so where no coördination of public and private activity has yet been brought about, and the fact that the modern welfare problem is essentially a complicated one requiring for its solution the help of many agencies, both public and private, these facts combine to demonstrate the necessity in any large city for the organization of a public welfare clearing house, such as is found in the modern Department of Public Welfare.

FUNCTIONS AND PURPOSE OF MODERN PUBLIC WELFARE WORK

Before the organization of a modern Department of Public Welfare is outlined, the functions and purpose of such departments, as seen in the experience of large cities in the United States that have established them, will be indicated.

The concept of public welfare has developed out of municipal and state activities concerning charities and corrections. At first the unemployed, destitute, pauper, idiotic, insane, blind, deaf, crippled, criminal and diseased were indiscriminately herded into public almshouses and jails. Then various forms of specialized institutions arose for caring for some of these unfortunates; others were placed under the control of the public health power which came to receive recognition later. Still other phases of charities and corrections remained, however, and the term public welfare has come to be applied to this residuum.

But the development has been by no means uniform. The "residuum" has varied from state to state and city to city, so that today in cities of the United States that have organized Departments of Public Welfare, such diverse functions are comprehended as caring for the destitute and the aged; caring for law-breakers, crippled, insane, epileptic, and feeble-minded; operating legal aid bureaus, lodging houses and employment bureaus; caring for abandoned, neglected, illegitimate and delinquent children; inspecting private welfare agencies, tenement houses, and commercial amusements; running playgrounds, band concerts, social centers, summer camps, comfort stations, public baths, community festivals; and carrying on research into problems of public welfare and the causes of delinquency and public dependency.

Some of these diversified functions assumed by municipal public welfare departments throughout the country logically belong to private philanthropy or to other city departments, so that the first task of any city undertaking to organize a Department of Public Welfare is to determine what its policy shall be in this respect, which functions it shall assume and which it shall leave for other departments and agencies. The following major groupings, however, are coming to be recognized as belonging to the field of public welfare administration:

(a) Public care for destitute families and individuals who are unemployable and who cannot be cared for by private agencies. In this division comes the work of the overseer of the poor and the superintendent of the almshouse. The tendency here is to refer all cases possible to specialized private agencies, to encourage old-age pensions for the aged, and to rehabilitate the infirm; i.e., the emphasis today is on prevention and reconstruction.

(b) Public aid for the unemployed and homeless. Here the municipal employment bureau is the natural clearing house; and the tendency is to operate some form of municipal work, such as a rock quarry, for those of the able-bodied needy

for whom no other employment can be found, to
pay for such work only in the form of meals, lodgings and grocery tickets, for the purpose of dis-
couraging too general a use of this form of emergency employment, and to urge the postponement
of necessary public work until times of unemployment crises. The modern method is to avoid
shifting unemployment to charity or to taxation
if at all possible.

(c) Public concern in cases of neglected, abandoned and delinquent children. Here the city
home should be the natural laboratory for a study
into causes of delinquency in which neglect and
abandonment are now recognized as playing a
major part.

(d) Public provision for recreation, and supervision of commercialized amusements. Under this
heading, the close relationship between improper
amusements and vice and delinquency is becoming
increasingly recognized, and this has led to the
licensing and inspecting of commercialized amusements in many cities. On the constructive side,
the tendency is to provide wholesome recreation
through public playgrounds, parks, baths, summer
camps, band concerts, and the like. Even though
parks and playgrounds may be in part administered under other city departments, the tendency
is to look to the Department of Public Welfare
for plans and constructive suggestions regarding
their use and supervision.

(e) Research into public welfare problems, and calling urgent needs to public attention.

A comparison of these groupings of public welfare function with the groupings in the field of private welfare brings out the parallel between them. In each group, where public welfare administration leaves off and private welfare administration begins is not easy to discern. This, in fact, is one of the first problems to be worked out by a city organizing a Department of Public Welfare, and each individual city must solve it in accordance with its peculiar situation. The problem cannot be solved offhand, but must be worked out after consultation and study through the combined efforts of all the welfare interests affected, both public and private.

The purpose behind modern public welfare administration, already indicated in the foregoing description of its functions, can now be broadly summarized. Public welfare aims to be a definite service of democratic government, along with public health, public education, and public protection. While caring for those who have become public charges, it strives to effect efficient methods for rehabilitating the down and out, for equalizing opportunity for the socially unfortunate and deficient, for preventing individual and family disaster, and for building up a wholesome community atmosphere for all.

ORGANIZATION OF A MODERN DEPARTMENT OF PUBLIC WELFARE

Coming now to the organization of a modern Department of Public Welfare, it can be emphasized at the outset that this should begin at the top and not at the bottom. It has been shown several times already that one of the first problems to be solved is that of formulating a logical division of labor between public and private welfare administration to the end that duplication and waste may be eliminated. In this respect, as already indicated, each city has its own peculiar situation. State laws, municipal ordinances, established local traditions, the particular lines of development in the local field of private welfare—these and other factors will determine the division of effort finally formulated, and this can be accomplished only after concerted study and planning by all the local interests concerned.

Advisory Board or Commission: It will be necessary, therefore, to do what many cities have done in this matter; namely, establish an advisory board or commission representative of the community and the welfare interests of the city. This advisory board,[1] appointed by the Mayor, should

---

[1] The question of whether such a board should be temporary and transitional or permanent and vested with certain legislative powers need not concern us here. Neither need the question of whether the members of the board should ultimately be appointed by the Mayor or be provided for in some other way. These are important questions, but they need not be settled at the outset of establishing a Department of Public Welfare. In the organization stage, the Public Welfare Board or Commission should be purely advisory and responsible to the Mayor, with whom the success or failure of the new department would normally rest.

be large enough to adequately represent the general citizenship and all important welfare interests but not so large as to be unwieldy. A body of from ten to fifteen members would probably answer the purpose all around.

In general the functions of the advisory board would be as follows:

(a) The elimination of duplication between city and private welfare administration and the working out of a logical division of labor between them;

(b) Securing the coöperation of both public and private agencies in working out the welfare problems of the city;

(c) Securing adequate public support and appreciation of the work of the Department of Public Welfare;

(d) Urging upon private agencies the need of economizing and strengthening their work through membership in a general federation, seeing to it that the confidential exchange of information regarding welfare cases is dependable and worthy of the confidence of all, public and private agencies alike, and insisting upon some plan of charities endorsement which will eliminate unworthy and fraudulent activities and assure public confidence in those endorsed;

(e) The visualization of the welfare problem of the community in its entirety and offering advice and suggestions from time to time on further welfare activities to be undertaken, either by private agencies or by the city.

The advisory board should be equally representative of private welfare agencies (through men officially connected with them) and of the public (through representative business men and social workers). It should be wholly advisory in character, and should do its work through sub-committees dealing with important welfare problems (such as family relief, unemployment, child welfare, recreation). These sub-committees should report from time to time to the advisory board, the reports serving as a basis for the formulation of the board's general policy. The Director of Public Welfare, or a representative of the city bureau concerned, and representatives of the private agencies most active in the particular field, should be on each sub-committee.

The Director of Public Welfare should also be named secretary of the Mayor's advisory board so that he can always be in a position to take active part in its work, and the advisory board should meet at the call of the Mayor, the Director of Public Welfare, or the chairman of the board.

How the sub-committees would function can be made clear through an illustration, taking the sub-committee on family welfare as an example. In ascertaining how far there had been duplication of effort and conflict with respect to family relief and what division of responsibility might be undertaken, consideration could be given to those cases of family need, known to several private agencies and to the overseer of the poor, in which no progress had been made and no responsibility for relief had apparently been assumed. An examination of such cases would afford a basis for working out a division of responsibility with respect to family relief. Other sub-committees could follow a similar procedure.

Office of the Director of Public Welfare: Turning to the office of the Director of Public Welfare and to the organization of his department, it will have been noted that the director would have a two-fold relationship,—one to the Mayor's advisory board, as its secretary and as represented on its sub-committees, and the other as executive head of the Department of Public Welfare. In the one relationship, the director's office would be serving the advisory board and its sub-committees; in the other relationship the director would be directing and coördinating the activities of the various bureaus falling within the scope of his department, i.e. the Bureau of the Overseer of the Poor, the Almshouse, the Employment Bureau, the City Home for Delinquent Children, the summer Camp, the Public Baths, and the Band Concerts, or any other activities being carried on by the municipality.

There is no reason why the heads of these various bureaus should be disturbed. Each should continue with his work much as before, with the exception that he would report and be responsible to the Director of Public Welfare, who in turn would be responsible to the Mayor. Where necessary the work of the various bureaus should of course be modernized and up-to-date business methods should prevail throughout, but no material structural changes need be made until a working policy had been formulated for the entire department. As already indicated, the working out of this policy in conjunction with the advisory board would take time, and in its formulation the various bureau heads should have a voice. A year or more would elapse before the policy became effective, so that the question of developing or changing the work of any bureau of the department would not arise until later. What direction this development might take has already been indicated elsewhere.

At the beginning, therefore, in addition to the appointment and organization of the advisory board, the other important organization detail applies to the office of the director. The director's office, in collaboration with the advisory board, should constitute the seat of clearing-house activity and the center of coördinating effort as between the departmental bureaus themselves, between the Department of Public Welfare and other departments of the city government, and between the Department and private welfare

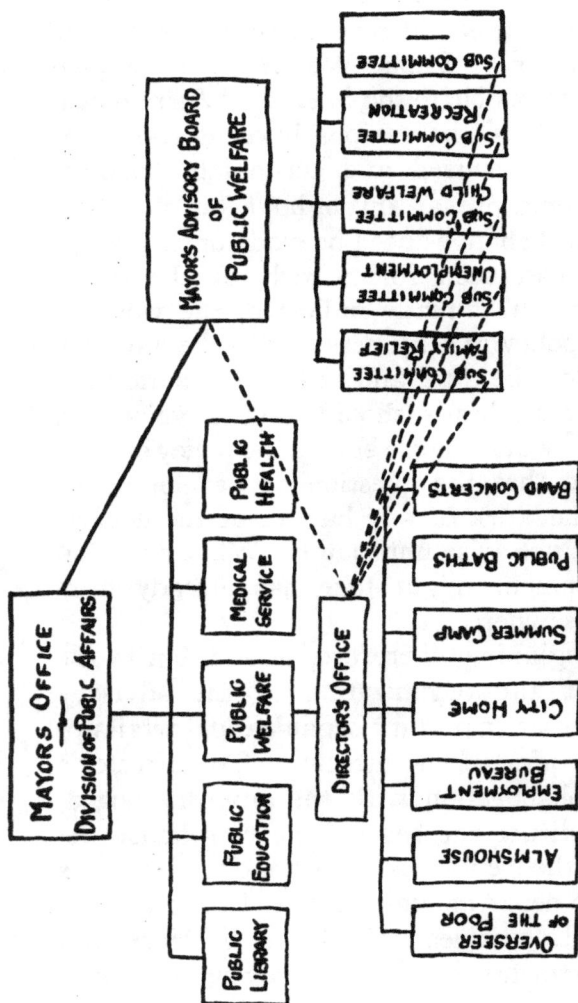

ORGANIZATION CHART
MODERN DEPARTMENT OF PUBLIC WELFARE

JOSEPH MAYER, 1923.

agencies. All questions of relief and coöperation would be directed to this office through which they would be referred to the proper bureau, department, or agency.

The actual clearing-house routine would be somewhat as follows: Applications for relief would come either directly from needy families or individuals or would be referred by some city department, such as the Department of Health, or by a private welfare agency. A record would be made, not to duplicate or supersede the complete detailed records kept by the bureaus or agencies working on the case, but of a nature suitable to clearing-house purposes, indicating particularly the agencies interested, character of aid received, what investigations or actions are under way with respect thereto, what further aid is contemplated, and the agency taking responsible charge. The card containing this record would be kept in the active file until disposition of the case, when the nature of the final disposition would be recorded.

The importance of a trustworthy confidential exchange is seen right here. The Director of Public Welfare would naturally wish to turn to such an exchange for information, provided he had confidence in its reliability. If the exchange is not functioning properly, this would be one of the first questions the advisory board and the Director of Public Welfare would wish to take up.

Returning to the clearing-house activities of the director's office, for the first year at least the director will be working out the problems involved as he goes along and will doubtless wish to keep this work under his immediate supervision. The personnel he will need, besides his secretary, who will have additional duties to those involved in the clearing-house activities, should not exceed a file clerk and one or two investigators. However, as these clearing-house activities develop, the logical outgrowth is a departmental Bureau of Research, if this is not already in existence. The development in one large city in this respect was as follows: first, registration of clearing-house cases; then, survey of the city's public welfare needs; later, more extended investigations into particular welfare problems; and, finally, the establishment of a Bureau of Research.

The attached organization chart covers in general outline the organization suggestions made in this section. A glance at the chart will show how this plan of municipal public welfare activities could be employed in other cities without changing the plan of organization here set forth. In short, the plan can be made to apply to the public welfare needs of almost any large American city.

ADVANTAGES AND ECONOMIES

The advantages and economies to be expected from the organization of a municipal Department of Public Welfare built along modern lines have been indicated in a number of places in the preceding sections of this article. Here it will suffice to bring them together in a brief summary statement.

Every American city of any considerable size aims to help its unfortunate and needy residents in some way. Year by year large sums of money are spent on temporary relief, jails, reformatories and other public charitable and correctional activities. The question is whether these expenditures and services are to be carried on under conditions that are necessarily wasteful, that force a competition with the splendid system of private relief built up in recent years, and that usually make for temporary rather than permanent assistance, or whether through the application of modern business methods a constructive and permanently beneficial service will be rendered.

The advantages and economies to be expected are seen in the elimination of the overlapping and wasteful duplication of effort otherwise existing between public and private welfare administration, in systematically and to the fullest extent utilizing the specialized resources of private philanthropy in the city in question, in protecting the public against the solicitation of unworthy and fraudulent charities, in assisting more of the needy in a constructive way while at the same time spending less for material relief, in conserving human life and keeping people from becoming destitute and out of almshouses in addition to giving what material help is necessary, in possibly cutting down the cost of maintenance of the city home and almshouse through the application of modern methods, in developing a plan involving the mobilization of all related agencies to combat unemployment both in its ordinary proportions and as brought on by industrial depression, in preventing the usual shift of unemployment to charity and the taxpayer, in constructively protecting childhood against neglect and unwholesome surroundings and thus lessening destitution and criminality in later years, in protecting the youth of the city from dangerous and improper amusements and furnishing needed recreational facilities to serve the welfare of all citizens, in keeping pace with modern developments in the welfare field and in applying preventative measures to avoid foreseeable dangers before they arise. In brief, the advantages and economies growing out of the organization of a modern Department of Public Welfare result from building up and offering a constructive and coördinated service of rehabilitation, conservation, and community well-being for all, and at the same time eliminating overlapping, duplication, and that useless expenditure for material relief which renders no constructive assistance.

CHAPTER XII

PLANNING POWERS OF MASSACHUSETTS DEPARTMENTS

MOST people think of planning as a new power for a state department and few realize the extent of the work Massachusetts, through her state departments, has already done in this field. The history of the growth of this work points to a gradually increasing recognition of problems and a desire to meet these problems in a scientific way. As the civic consciousness is awakened to the need of far-sighted planning public opinion is created and legislative action results. The first legislative act to grant planning powers to a state department in Massachusetts recognized the dangers of grade crossings and sought to lessen accidents from this cause. The problem of transporting people and goods safely and conveniently has long been a recognized problem. Realization of the effects localities have on the health of the people brought more legislation, to be followed by acts concerning the purity of the water supply, drainage and sewage disposal. Soon it became evident that laws were needed to ensure protection from fire to persons employed in large numbers under one roof; that laws were needed, also, to protect the public from poorly built theatres, halls and other public buildings; and that some state supervision was needed to ensure even decently wholesome living conditions for the people of the commonwealth.

PUBLIC UTILITIES

In 1864 the Board of Railroad Commissioners was formed, its chief duties at that time being to make grade crossings more safe. The Board of Gas Commissioners was established in 1885. From these beginnings was evolved our present Department of Public Utilities with its powers of supervision over such chartered public utility corporations as gas and electric companies, water companies, railroad corporations, street railway companies and telephone and telegraph companies. There are engaged in some form of public utility operation under the jurisdiction of the department 366 companies, persons, associations and municipalities. The department studies the problems of these companies and gives assistance where possible to them and to the public served by them. Special investigations and reports to the legislature are made when necessary, complaints received and hearings held. A special report of the department to the legislature on transpo. ˗tion facilities in the metropolitan district is of great interest, resulting, as it did, in the formation of a Division of Metropolitan Planning in the Metropolitan District Commission.

HIGHWAY AND HARBOR PLANNING

The Department of Public Works grew from the Board of Harbor Commissioners established in 1866 and the Massachusetts Highway Commission established in 1893. It now has two divisions with planning powers clearly established,—the Division of Highways and the Division of Waterways and Public Lands.

The Division of Highways is empowered to advise and coöperate with local governments in the construction of public ways; to maintain and repair state highways, to erect guide-posts, to care for trees, and to prepare highway maps; to regulate billboards; to collect information relative to the geological formation of the commonwealth, so far as it relates to materials for road-building; and to take land by eminent domain on behalf of the Commonwealth. In addition to its work of road-building, widening, tree-planting, and advice to municipalities, the Division of Highways has drawn up a five-year program for highway work and a program for strengthening or rebuilding the many inadequate bridges of the state. At the end of the year 1922 the total length of state highways was 1,440.121 miles. For construction of state highways alone $2,883,592.54 was spent in 1922. The division has made rules and regulations for the control of billboards, has issued licenses and permits and has set apart four scenic highways on which billboards will be forbidden.

Out of 17 local ordinances and by-laws submitted by cities and towns, two have received the approval of the division.

The Division of Waterways and Public Lands is empowered to take charge of the lands, rights in lands, flats, shores and all rights in tide waters belonging to the commonwealth; to develop Boston harbor; to improve and preserve rivers and harbors; and to take and hold real estate and build thereon, and to lease wharves and piers. Work of this division includes pier improvement, filling and improvement of flats, harbor dredging, river improvement and shore protection by sea-walls. Reclamation of the province lands is being carried on. A study has been made of the great ponds in the commonwealth not under the jurisdiction of any other state department.

PLANNING FOR HEALTH

The importance of health was early recognized and the Board of Health and Vital Statistics was established in 1869. The act establishing this board read in part as follows: "They shall make sanitary investigations and inquiries in respect to the people, the causes of disease, and especially of epidemics and the sources of mortality and the effects of localities, employments, conditions and circumstances on the public health." Through various stages this board has developed into the Department of Public Health. Its powers, so far as they relate to planning include: sanitary investigations and inquiries relative to the causes of diseases, the sources of mortality and the effects of localities, etc., on the public health; examination annually of all main outlets of sewers and drainage of towns of the commonwealth, and the effect of sewage disposal; making of rules for the sanitary protection of waters used for water supply; and advising municipalities with reference to water supply, drainage and sewerage.

The following are among the recent accomplishments of the department in carrying out these duties: a three-years' investigation of the water supply needs of the commonwealth by this department and the Metropolitan District Commission which resulted in important recommendations; advice given to cities and towns with reference to water supply, ice supply, sewerage and pollution of streams; assistance given to the State Reclamation Board in connection with plans for the drainage of wet lands; study of sewerage systems; study of nuisances caused by oil refineries; and study of the purification of wastes from industrial works and their effect on streams.

PLANNING FOR SAFETY

In 1877 inspection of public buildings was made one of the duties of the state detective force established in 1865. Interest at that time centered largely in means of egress in case of fire and protection of employees from dangerous machinery. Here is found the germ of the present Department of Public Safety with its Division of Inspection and its Division of Fire Prevention. The Division of Inspection supervises plans and construction of public buildings; inspects public buildings and enforces laws regarding them; licenses theatres and inspects elevators. State building inspectors may be called upon by cities and towns having no inspector to inspect buildings which have been reported dangerous. The Division of Fire Prevention investigates causes of fires; makes rules for the removal of combustible materials likely to cause fires, rules for keeping of explosives; and studies fire hazard and fire protection and makes suggestions for the improvement of laws.

The Division of Inspection is under the charge of a director known as the Chief of Inspections. The buildings which come under the regulation of this department are of a public or semi-public nature and include public buildings, theatres, halls, churches, schools, places of assembly and places of public resort, factories, hotels, lodging and apartment houses and buildings containing eight or more rooms above the second floor occupied for either business or habitation.

The Division of Fire Prevention is under the charge of a director known as the State Fire Marshal who is also Fire Prevention Commis-

sioner for the metropolitan district. All fires in
the city of Boston and all incendiary fires or fires
of unknown origin occurring throughout the state
are investigated. Duties include also enforcement of rules and regulations pertaining to gar-
ages, explosives, fireworks and volatile inflamma-
ble liquids and compounds. The last report of the
Department of Public Safety states that loss by
fire is annually increasing in this commonwealth
and offers better building construction as one
means of reducing fire hazard.

METROPOLITAN PLANNING

The Metropolitan District Commission was
formed by uniting three separate commissions;—
the Metropolitan Sewerage Commission established in 1889, the Metropolitan Park Commission established in 1893, and the Metropolitan
Water Board established in 1895. The sewerage
district includes 26 municipalities in which the
Commission is charged with the construction and
maintenance of a sewerage system. The water
district includes 19 municipalities. Within this
district is maintained a system of metropolitan
water works. The parks district includes 37 municipalities within which the Metropolitan District
Commission may take or acquire lands for reser-
vation, boulevards and parkways. This year was
enacted an important piece of legislation affecting
metropolitan planning when the Division of

Metropolitan Planning was formed within the Metropolitan District Commission. This action is the result of a growing traffic and transportation problem and recognition of the fact that means must be found of solving this problem. The Division of Metropolitan Planning is empowered to investigate transportation service and facilities within a metropolitan district including 39 municipalities, confer with the planning boards, and recommend methods of executing and paying for the same.

The work of this Commission shows that much has been done toward metropolitan planning along certain lines. In an area of about 400 square miles there is a park area of 14 square miles. The parks and boulevards include about 106 miles of carriage roads; six beaches, with a total frontage of 13 miles; more than 53 miles of river banks; four bath-houses; the Charles river and Cradock bridge dams and locks; and the Boston and Cambridge embankments. The commission maintains and protects from pollution a water-supply for 19 municipalities and maintains and operates all the works for removing sewage from 26 municipalities. It is hoped that the new Division of Metropolitan Planning will do much toward the solution of the traffic and transportation problem of the district.

ABANDONED FARMS

In 1891 there was passed an act to authorize the State Board of Agriculture to collect and circulate information relating to abandoned farms. Duties were to collect all necessary information in regard to the opportunities for developing the agricultural resources of the commonwealth through the repopulation of abandoned or partially abandoned farms, and cause the facts obtained, and a statement of the advantages offered, to be circulated where and in such manner as the board considered for the best interests of the commonwealth. The board was authorized to spend $2,000 for this purpose.

The work is now a duty of the Division of Information of the Department of Agriculture. A list of farms for sale is maintained by the division for the use of people interested, the majority of inquiries coming from families of limited means who desire to live outside the city limits.

FOREST PLANNING

The Division of Forestry was formed within the Department of Conservation in 1904. It was entrusted with the duties of promoting the perpetuation, extension and proper management of the public and private forest lands of the commonwealth; replanting and management of all forest lands of the commonwealth; advising forest owners; purchasing land for experiment and illustration in forest management; purchase or taking of land for state forests; and providing seedlings for town forests.

About twenty years ago in Massachusetts the practice of scientific forestry as a state work was begun. The importance of this work is pointed out in the last report of the Department of Conservation, in which appears the following statement: "In Massachusetts we have more than a million acres of non-agricultural lands suitable only for forest growth that can be made to yield enormous profits, but do not. A liberal forestry program contemplates the utilization of these lands for the production of commercial trees." That this work is needed is emphasized by the statement that whereas once Massachusetts produced from her own soil all the timber she used she now imports 80 per cent of the amount used. Protection of forests from fire is a part of the work of the division and 39 observation stations are maintained from which the whole forest area of the state may be surveyed. This forest area covers a little over 52,000 acres and is being added to yearly. State plantations and nurseries are maintained and educational work is also carried on by the department.

IMPROVEMENT OF LOW LANDS AND SWAMPS

For the improvement of low lands a State Reclamation Board has been formed by act of the legislature in 1923 consisting of one member of the Department of Public Health and one member of the Department of Agriculture. Duties of this board include: investigation of the question of utilizing the wet lands to ascertain what lands may advantageously be drained for agricultural or industrial uses, for the protection of the public health, for the utilization of deposits therein, or for other purposes. This board was previously called the State Drainage Board, the formation of which, in 1918, was the result of a report made at the request of the legislature the preceding year. Before this, in 1913, the State Board of Agriculture and the State Board of Health acting as a joint board were authorized, with the approval of the governor and council, to purchase or take by right of eminent domain wet lands to be drained, reclaimed and cultivated. Before the enactment of this measure improvement of low lands was brought about by petition of the proprietors and appointment by the courts of commissioners to carry on the work.

HOUSING

Interest in housing and in ventilation and sanitation provisions is fairly recent, not receiving legislative recognition until 1912 when the permissive state tenement house act for towns was passed, followed in 1913 by the state tenement house act for cities and the establishment of the Homestead Commission. The state tenement house acts cannot properly be included under the heading "State Planning" as they are subject to local acceptance and local administration. The Homestead Commission is now known as the Division of Housing and Town Planning of the Department of Public Welfare. Its duties are as follows: to investigate defective housing, the evils resulting therefrom and the remedies; to study the operation of building laws and laws relating to tenement houses; to promote the formation of organizations intended to increase the number of wholesome homes for the people; and to encourage the creation of local planning boards, gather information for their use and for the use of city governments and selectmen in towns. It has power, with the consent of the governor and council, to take land, and build and sell houses for the purpose of relieving congestion.

In the performance of its duties the division has recently made a study of the building and housing laws of the commonwealth finding three kinds of codes: building codes which regulate materials of construction and give some degree of fire protection; tenement house acts which cover tenement houses only, but which make some provision for light and air, size of rooms, privacy and sanitation; and housing codes which make these provisions for all dwellings. Results showed 20 cities and towns protected by building laws only; 14 with tenement house acts; 4 with housing codes and 25 cities and towns which have accepted the state tenement house act.

The division keeps in close touch with and assists as much as possible the 62 active planning boards in the state. To help in this work a new position has been created, that of State Consultant on Housing and Town Planning. The creation of new boards is encouraged and information on housing and town planning gathered and disseminated.

HOUSING AND RENTS

To deal with the recent and widespread rent increase a temporary commission known as the Commission on the Necessaries of Life was created by act of the legislature in 1919. This commission was established for the term of one year but each year has been granted another year of life as the need for it continues to exist. The commission deals with rent and eviction problems. In carrying out its duties it has made a study of the extent of the housing shortage in Massachusetts and has acted as a go-between for landlords and tenants during the housing emergency. Evils which the commission has tried to combat include the prohibition of children from rented houses; the summary eviction of tenants; and unjust and exorbitant increases in rents.

For about sixty years Massachusetts has been developing her planning powers. The growth has constantly been toward a more definite policy of comprehensive planning. First the state concerned itself with such matters as safety of grade crossings and means of egress from public buildings in case of fire, gradually extending her powers to include more definite planning such as far-sighted programs of highway development, forest preservation and extension and reclamation of wet lands. Two important steps were taken in 1923. One was the formation within the Metropolitan District Commission of the Division of Metropolitan Planning which will work for the improvement and coördination of transportation facilities for an area including thirty-seven cities and towns. The other legislative acts of 1923 which will have a direct influence on the planning work throughout the whole state authorized the appointment in the Division of Housing and Planning of a State Consultant whose duties will include advising and coöperating with the sixty-two local planning boards already functioning, the carrying on of educational work and a campaign to stimulate interest and action in places where no planning is being done.

CHAPTER XIII

A FEDERAL DEPARTMENT OF
PUBLIC WELFARE

A N important phase of the public welfare movement in the United States is that centering around the proposal for a Federal Department. While this movement seems somewhat delayed at the present time, its consideration will prove an important element in the discussions of the public welfare as related to state and local departments. Here again there is great diversity of views, difference of opinions, and varied interpretations of the scope and purpose of a federal department of public welfare. For the most part, students of social science and public welfare have shown little interest in the movement and have troubled little to improve conditions.

An exception to this rule, however, is found in the concrete discussion of Robert W. Kelso, former commissioner of public welfare of Massachusetts, Richard K. Conant, present commissioner of public welfare, Sanford Bates, and Herbert A. Parsons, of the state department of public welfare in Massachusetts. Mr. Kelso and Mr. Conant present the arguments for a federal department. Mr. Bates and Mr. Parsons present the arguments against the department. These papers are reproduced from the *Journal of Social Forces* and were the result of a radio debate and therefore should be read with this in mind holding the authors responsible for these views only as they represent a formal statement representative of the subject. They are given in this volume because they represent the clearest and most informing discussion which we have seen on the subject.

A second type of source material in which those who are interested in public welfare may judge of the scope and purpose of federal departments will be found in typical bills which have been presented or proposed. Whether this legislation will ever be enacted or not, it is important in indicating the scope of the subject, certain forms of reorganization, as well as difficulties in the way of effective legislation. They are also representative of the difficulties involved in such legislation and reorganization. The two outstanding proposed bills are therefore included in this chapter.

EVIDENCE FOR A FEDERAL DEPARTMENT

Mr. Robert W. Kelso presents certain arguments for a state department: "At the outset of this discussion we learn that the elements of a Department of Public Welfare proposed by the affirmative are already in existence—a Children's Bureau; a Bureau of Education; a Division of Indian Affairs; a Public Health Service. But these elements, instead of being arranged coherently under one head are at present scattered among existing departments just as they happened to grow. One is in the Department of Labor; another in the Treasury; still others in the Department of the Interior. Each must wait for the consideration of its problems until the more pressing affairs of the department have been attended to, and none has representation or opportunity for the consideration of its pressing matters in the cabinet.

"It is my share in the discussion to point out to you the reason why these scattered bureaus have grown up. That reason constitutes a complete answer to the contention of our opponent who has just preceded me. He says, you know, that charity like crime is local, and that the national government should not meddle in matters which apply to the states. On the score of meddling we believe him to be altogether sound. In his view of charity we think he is mediaeval. For the charity which he has in mind is only that old-time phase of personal, friendly, neighborly relief to persons in distress. Charity in the sense in which we must use the word in this discussion regarding the Public Welfare is to be defined as social service, a thing of vastly greater import and infinitely more far-reaching in consequence. The various public welfare bureaus now scattered through our Washington machinery have arisen out of the very fact that charity in its social service meaning has ceased to be local. They are eloquent evidence of the truth that the public welfare of your city or mine, of your county or mine, of your state or mine, has become definitely and forever the concern and the problem of the whole people.

"It is not so many decades ago that the people of the United States lived an agricultural life, and many of them were frontiersmen. We were a country of distances. So recent is it that space and the seasons of the year were a serious obstacle to getting together, that we still inaugurate our president on the 4th day of March, that representing the winter traveling-time to the capital. It is only a little while ago that we had no railroads, no steamships, no telephone, no telegraph, no regular mail delivery, and very little in the way of a weekly let alone a daily press.

"Now those days have gone. We have more railroad mileage than all the rest of the world. We have the telephone in almost every household. We have steamships, reducing the old six-weeks voyage across the Atlantic to less than one week. We have even an aerial mail service; and as we stand here at Medford Hillside speaking, somewhere between 700,000 and 1,000,000 persons scattered from London to the Rocky Mountains, and from the Arctic to South America, are listening. We have eliminated space and time to such a degree that the world of today is no longer even similar to the world of a decade ago.

"So great is the advance in chemistry, in physics, in industrial development, that the production of goods definitely approaches a great unit basis of operation; wherefore we build mighty cities about a single industry. And thinking so hard about the making of goods and the earning of dollars, we forget so to build those cities that play, which is the real business of childhood, is provided for, and family groups are herded together in cramped quarters with a view only to the economy of operation. So intensive is this movement in industry that human beings are arranged almost like spools upon a spinning frame to whirl about, each one with his distinct set of motions, hour after hour, day in and day out, year in and year out, all of them links in the long chain of production.

"We have ceased to be a vast land dotted with households occupied by individuals isolated from each other. We have become one mighty people, with interests so closely and so vitally inter-related that the ill-health of one is the misfortune of another; that the ignorance of your child is the drawback of mine; that the welfare of one town or one city, or one district can in no wise be injured without hurting the whole.

"Shall we say then that such mighty problems as the conservation of child life, the treatment of women in industry, the sound standards of city building for purposes of sanitation and the protection of health, and the provision of public schooling for youth, are nevertheless the exclusive business of our smallest units of government? The truth is that they are not; and that as a people we recognize the fact that they are not—recognize it so completely that with all our jealousy of federal development we nevertheless find the need of establishing a bureau which shall develop and is now effectually developing standards of child care and child treatment. We have a federal Department of Education which must develop standards of public educational service. We have a public health service which must lead the nation in that mighty educational campaign which shall change the conception of ill-health into the philosophy of health itself. And if my line of reasoning is sound, it must follow that these nation-wide problems will continue to press harder in the future than they have in the past. The time has gone by for the old colonial conception of departmental organization and the time has arrived—indeed it is overdue—for the arrangement of our government service in the light of present-day national needs. With all due respect to my learned opponent I remind him that charity once was the business of a few self-appointed philanthropists, but that social work is the business of democracy. This is the essential difference between the olden times and the new. It is the case for the affirmative that we meet the new need with new machinery. And lest our opponents feel that we are alone in our point of view, I take the liberty of quoting from a learned authority in constitutional law, the President of the United States, who in his first great message to Congress said this:

"For purposes of national uniformity we ought to provide, by Constitutional Amendment and appropriate legislation, for a limitation of child labor, and in all cases, under exclusive jurisdiction of the federal government a minimum wage law for women.

"I do not favor the making of appropriations from the National Treasury to be expended directly on local education, but I do consider it a fundamental requirement of national activity which, accompanied by allied subjects of welfare, is worthy of a separate department and a place in the cabinet."

Continuing the affirmative *Mr. Richard K. Conant* argues that: "Throughout the nation, the cities and the states have their departments of public welfare, but there is no national Department of Public Welfare at Washington. The Public Health Service is in the Treasury Department, the Children's Bureau is in the Department of Labor, the Bureau of Education finds lodgings in the Department of the Interior.

"Our late President, Warren G. Harding, in his msesage to Congress early in 1921, said—'In the realms of education, public health, sanitation, conditions of workers in industry, child welfare, proper amusement and recreation, the elimination of social vice and many other subjects, the government has already undertaken a considerable range of activities—but these undertakings have been scattered through many departments and bureaus without coördination and with much overlapping of functions which fritters energies and magnifies the cost. To bring these various activities together in a single department, where the whole field could be surveyed, and where their interrelationships could be properly appraised, would make for increased effectiveness, economy and intelligence of direction.'

"Social service has become so widespread in this country that in a single state—Massachusetts —it is carried on by over 1,000 private charitable corporations, expending over 33 million dollars a year; it is carried on by 355 cities and towns, and by the commonwealth in its State Department of Public Welfare, which has supervision over 80,-000 persons. I can assure you that the 48 states are tackling these tremendous problems in at least 48 different ways. There is a crying need for a central federal department which, while it need not duplicate any of the work of the separate states, can guide them and make available to them the experience of all the states and of foreign countries. Great preventive movements in social service develop from such combined research and combined activity. Such a field is properly the field of the Federal Government which has for one of the objects of its Constitution—'to promote the general welfare.'

"The government should pay as much attention to protecting childhood in its right to health, happiness and education; as much attention to the best methods of caring for disease and poverty, to the protection of women, to the care of the aged, and to the far-reaching preventive measures in health, sanitation, recreation, and mental hygiene as it does to the development of the navy, the distribution of seeds, the raising of cattle and the maintenance of armies.

"Public Welfare has become an important part of nearly every subordinate government organization within the United States. Let us follow President Harding's vision and make the nation's public welfare work more intelligent and more effective by creating a federal department, a department of the central government of the whole United States."

EVIDENCE AGAINST A FEDERAL DEPARTMENT

Turning to the other side *Mr. Sanford Bates* presents five arguments against a centralized department of public welfare: "My colleague and I wish it distinctly understood that nothing which we may say is to be interpreted as any argument against the necessity for scientific social work. We are hoping to be able to demonstrate to you, however, that the federal government would not

improve matters by establishing a separate De- ·
partment of Public Welfare with a cabinet officer
at its head.

1. "Such a department is unconstitutional.
While it may not be popular to refer to the Constitution with those who are impatient to bring in
the millennium in social reform, nevertheless it is
wise to make sure before we commit ourselves to
the advocacy of a Federal Department of Public
Welfare, that such a step would be supported by
our highest court, as a legitimate exercise of
federal government. It is common knowledge to
every school boy that the seat of all sovereignty
over our people is with the several states, that the
basis of the federal government is a delegation of
certain specified powers by the states to the national government and that the document which
measures the extent of those delegated powers is
the Constitution of the United States. Unless we
can find, therefore, in the language of that historic
document either express or implied delegation to
Congress to do a certain act, the exercise of any
such authority is unwarranted.

"The preamble of the Constitution does refer to
the promotion of the public welfare in general
terms. By many judicial decisions, however, the
preamble forms no part of the binding Constitution. Apart from this statement, no mention is
made anywhere in the Constitution that the states
intended to give up certain of their sovereign

rights, among them the duty of caring for the welfare of their own citizens. Section 8 of Article 1 defines the powers of Congress as delegated by the states. The fiscal, commercial, martial, jurisdictional limitations of its power are therein enumerated, but nowhere does it refer to charity, correction or social endeavor, of any sort. The 'elastic clause' of the Constitution, so-called, which has by judicial decision been stretched to the breaking point, and which gives Congress the power to make laws which shall be necessary and proper for carrying into execution the foregoing powers, can hardly be invoked to warrant a federated government caring for the work of public relief and re-habilitation.

2. "It follows, therefore, that legally as well as logically, the states should retain the control over concerns of public welfare. Legally, because the Constitution requires it, and logically because, after all, states differ greatly in population, topography, customs, tradition and temperaments. A law which would be suitable for Massachusetts would not do for Mississippi. What would be fair in Montana might not be in Michigan. Public aid and relief, laws governing poverty, infirmity and delinquency are local in nature, applied in smaller compass, and can be most efficiently, economically and humanely administered by state governments.

3. "And speaking of economy, hasn't the federal government about all it can do to make both

ends meet nowadays, without taking on any extra expenditures? Is there a citizen of the United States who isn't satisfied with the size of his federal tax bill, or who wants to see it any larger?

"In 1902 our federal government appropriated for its purposes seven hundred and seventy-nine millions of dollars, and in 1912 nine hundred and fifty-nine millions of dollars, and in 1922 $5,814,-000,000, which by the way was a considerable drop from the war record of 1919—$31,978,000,000.

"Furniture of all kinds is high in price, but the United States government bureaus still hold the record as the highest priced kind of furniture that I know anything about.

4. "Our federal government is the best in the world in many things, and not so good in others. It is splendid in its international affairs, as witness its action in dealing with the weaker countries, such as Cuba, Panama, Japan, China, etc. But it is not so good in its internal affairs. It is good at making war, but it spent a lot of money taking care of soldiers which never got to the soldiers. It passes a constitutional amendment to stop the sale and manufacture of booze, and we all say 'Amen' to that, but it does not stop the sale and manufacture of booze. Some of you no doubt who paid an income tax in 1918 and also paid a lawyer to make out a return for you, which he probably didn't understand, are just now even

finding out that you didn't pay enough and are being invited to pay some more. No, the experience of our government with its Veterans' Bureau, its prohibition enforcement and its income tax collection does not lead us to think that it would be a howling success in administering the difficult and arduous humanitarian tasks now so admirably handled by state and local public welfare departments.

5. "Do we need any more cabinet officers? Is there any man who knows enough about health, education, crime prevention, housing, children's work, aid and relief, etc., to be the final arbiter on all these questions? The nation's education people say 'No.' They want their own specialized department. The question of transportation many claim is large enough to warrant its having a department by itself. Public health workers, those interested in the delinquency problems and others have grave doubts as to the ability of any general welfare department to handle their particular problems. Until the need is more definitely established we should go slowly with any such proposition.

"Faith, hope and charity, says the Good Book and the greatest of these is charity, but charity finds its birth and growth in the individual human heart and it cannot be nurtured in officialdom. Let our government maintain armies, coin money, regulate the currency, provide a navy, carry our mails, collect duties and imports, maintain courts and dispense justice, but let us leave to our citizens and to our more compact and democratic divisions of government the bestowal of charity. In the same way that the individual unfortunate prefers the quiet friendly service from a private source or from some brother in misfortune to a public dispensation, so will the people of our country prefer that their contribution to charity be given out of a full and understanding heart and not through the medium of a tax bill."

Mr. Herbert A. Parsons closes the argument against a federal department: "The proposal we meet is one to create a new and great federal governmental machine. Are there not sufficient facilities for access to the United States Treasury? If not, then a Department of Welfare would be ideal. The name has a charm all its own. It carries an implication that if there is any direction in which the beneficence of government has not yet run,— or if there is any in which it has not flowed freely, —a channel is to be provided.

"The title has the further merit that it may mean anything,—not otherwise provided for; everything,—under a government that exists for general welfare; or nothing,—in any definite way.

"Into such a department, so labelled,. could be gathered all the welfare undertakings of the government. There is no existing department that has not its welfare features, related to its own service. To gather these into a department with welfare for its reason for existence is to accomplish two things:

(1) "To take the various services away from their traditional and natural setting, and

(2) "To dehumanize to that extent the departments in which there are now the expression of a relation of all government activities to the interests of humanity.

"There is nothing to indicate that these interests are not as well cared for in the departments to which they are now related as they possibly could be in one that was even more miscellaneous.

"It would indeed be a miscellaneous department, with interests very diverse and having no other bond than that of a sentimental interest.

"The first requisite of a new department of government is a distinct public interest with a view to expert direction. Such an interest, for example, is education. Some claim could be made to recognition of this concern of the nation with an educator at its head. Another is health. Its administrator would of necessity be a medical expert. Child care,—the protection of the child life of the nation,—is such a distinct interest.

"What is proposed is to bring together bureaus now eminently serving their objects under directors with expert qualifications and rolling them into one department,—under what sort of a secretarial chief? Is there the combination in one person of expertness in education, in medicine, in child care, in immigration, in conservation, in pure foods, in supervision of the Indians, in naturalization, in prisons,—to take a few out of the list of welfare bureaus that now scatter through the entire service?

"A case could be made out for a department of education, by far less able advocates than our opponents of this evening. The public interest here is a commanding one. It is capable of direction by a great educational authority. To merge it in a department of miscellaneous bureaus would be to defeat the end sought.

"Even as to a great special interest of the people it is a poor notion of government that in order to secure attention to it we must add to the group of the President's advisers. There is no indication that the President stands in need of advice. And none that any of the causes mentioned suffers neglect because he is not more fully advised.

"But public welfare, so far as it has a distinct meaning, relates to the extension of relief. To use it in relation to the national government is to invite the transfer of the powers reserved to the states to the nation. That policy is already under severe and justified criticism. Set up a department of public welfare and you run up the white flag of surrender of the rights most sacredly guarded by the constitution. You open wide the way to the conversion of the United States government into a machine of social care, for which it is unfitted and for which it was never designed.

"The proposal of such a department is the extreme height of that plea for bureaucratic government, which all the world's experience directs this American people to avoid."

PROPOSED LEGISLATION

Efforts to coördinate public welfare agencies and work at the National Capital have revealed unusual difficulties in organization, in morale, in political adaptations, and in social technique. What the exact outcome of proposed legislation will be is problematic but it is apparently clear that for a long time no comprehensive and adequate organization will emerge. Two major proposals are presented here to illustrate the direction of certain thought and effort and to challenge the student of social work, of public welfare, and of governmental efficiency to study more fully the situation and needs.

THE LATER BILL. *Be it enacted by the Senate and House of Representatives of the United States of America in Congress assembled,* That there is hereby established at the seat of government an executive department to be known as the Department of Education and Relief. The chief officer of the Department of Education and Relief, who shall have control and direction of said department, shall be appointed by the President, by and with the advice and consent of the Senate. He shall be known as the Secretary of Education and Relief, and shall receive a salary of $12,000 per annum. His term and tenure of office shall be the same as that of the heads of the other executive departments. Section 158 of the Revised Statutes is hereby amended to include the Department of Education and Relief, and the provisions of Title IV of the Revised Statutes, including all amendments thereto, are hereby made applicable to said department. The Secretary of Education and Relief shall cause a seal of office to be made for the Department of Education and Relief of such device as the President shall approve, and judicial notice shall be taken thereof.

Sec. 2. There shall be in the Department of Education and Relief three Assistant Secretaries, to be appointed by the President, by and with the advice and consent of the Senate. They shall be known, respectively, as the Assistant Secretary for Education, the Assistant Secretary for Public Health, and the Assistant Secretary for Veteran Relief. Each Assistant Secretary shall perform such duties as may be prescribed by the Secretary or required by law, and shall each receive a salary of $10,000 per annum. There shall also be a solicitor, a chief clerk, and a disbursing clerk, and such other officers and employees as may from time to time be authorized by Congress.

Sec. 3. It shall be the province and duty of the Department of Education and Relief to foster and promote public education and health, and the interests, as determined by law, of persons separated from the military or naval forces of the United States; and to this end it shall be vested with jurisdiction and control over the bureaus, offices, and branches of the public service hereinafter specified. All unexpended appropriations which shall be available at the time when this Act takes effect in relation to the various bureaus, offices, and branches of the public service which are by this Act transferred to or included in the Department of Education and Relief, or which are abolished by this Act, and their authority, powers, and duties transferred to the Department of Education and Relief, shall become available for expenditure by the Department of Education and Relief and shall be treated as if said branches of the public service had been directly named in the laws making said appropriations as parts of the Department of Education and Relief.

Sec. 4. (a) The Bureau of Pensions, the Bureau of Education, Saint Elizabeth's Hospital, Howard University, and

Freedmen's Hospital, and all pertaining thereto, are hereby transferred from the Department of the Interior to the Department of Education and Relief.

(b) The Public Health Service, including all that pertains thereto, is hereby transferred from the Department of the Treasury to the Department of Education and Relief.

(c) The Federal Board for Vocational Education is hereby abolished, and the authority, powers, and duties conferred and imposed by law upon such board shall be held, exercised, and performed by the Assistant Secretary for Education, under the general direction of the Secretary of Education and Relief.

(d) The office of Commissioner of Education is hereby abolished, and the authority, powers, and duties conferred and imposed by law upon the Commissioner of Education shall be held, exercised, and performed by the Assistant Secretary for Education, under the general direction of the Secretary of Education and Relief.

(e) The Assistant Secretary for Veteran Relief shall be ex officio a member of the Board of Managers of the National Home for Disabled Volunteer Soldiers; in addition to the members heretofore provided for by law; and all reports of expenditures and receipts, and all other reports required by law to be submitted by the Board of Managers, and all accounts and estimates of appropriations, shall be submitted to and supervised by the Secretary of Education and Relief, who shall transmit the same to Congress, to the General Accounting Office, or to the Bureau of the Budget, as may be required by law, together with any recommendation which he may deem proper.

(f) The authority, powers, and duties conferred and imposed by law upon the Secretary of the Interior with relation to the Columbia Institution for the Deaf, shall be held, exercised, and performed by the Secretary of Education and Relief; and the Assistant Secretary for Education shall be ex officio a director of such institution, in addition to the directors whose appointment has heretofore been provided by law.

(g) The United States Veterans' Bureau, including all that pertains thereto, is hereby transferred to and made a part of the Department of Education and Relief. The office of Director of the United States Veterans' Bureau is hereby abolished, and the authority, powers, and duties conferred and imposed by law upon the Director shall be held, exercised, and performed by the Assistant Secretary for Veteran Relief, subject to the general direction of the Secretary of Education and Relief: *Provided,* That the Assistant Secretary for Veteran Relief shall have final authority in the adjudication and settlement of any claim or other matter involving or affecting the rights and interests of any beneficiary of the United States Veterans' Bureau.

Sec. 5.   The official records and papers on file in and pertaining to the business of any bureau, office, or branch of the public service which is transferred by this Act to the Department of Education and Relief, or which is abolished by this Act and its authority, powers, and duties transferred to the Department of Education and Relief, together with the furniture, equipment, and other property in use in such bureau, office, or branch of the public service, are hereby transferred to the Department of Education and Relief.

Sec. 6.   The Secretary of Education and Relief shall have charge, in the buildings and premises occupied by or assigned to the Department of Education and Relief, of the library, furniture, fixtures, records, and other property pertaining to it or hereafter acquired for use in its business.   Until other quarters are provided, the Department of Education and Relief may occupy the buildings and premises occupied by the bureaus, offices, and branches of the public service which are by this Act transferred to or included in said department, or which are abolished by this act, and their authority, powers, and duties transferred to said department.   Except as otherwise provided by this Act, the officers and employees employed in or under the jurisdiction of any bureau, office, or branch of the public service which is by this Act transferred to or included in the Department of Education and Relief, or which is abolished by this Act and its authority, powers, and duties transferred to said department, are each and all hereby transferred to said department without change in classification or compensation.

Sec. 7.   Except as otherwise provided by this Act, all authority, powers, and duties held, exercised, and performed by the head of any executive department in and over any bureau, office, officer, or branch of the public service which is by this Act transferred to the Department of Education and Relief, or which is abolished by this Act and its authority, powers, and duties transferred to said department, or in and over any business arising therefrom or pertaining thereto, or in relation to the duties performed by and authority conferred by law upon such bureau, office, officer, or branch of the public service, whether of an appellate or revisory character or otherwise, shall be vested in and exercised and performed by the Secretary of Education and Relief: *Provided, however,* That this shall not be construed to affect the provisions of the Act approved August 18, 1894, entitled "An Act making appropriations for sundry civil expenses of the Government for the fiscal year ending June 30, 1895, and for other purposes," relating to the annual inspection of the National Home for Disabled Volunteer Soldiers under the direction of the Secretary of War.

Sec. 8. The Secretary of Education and Relief shall make annually, at the close of each fiscal year, a report in writing to Congress, giving an account of all moneys received and disbursed by him and his department, describing the work done by the department, and making such recommendations as he shall deem necessary for the effective performance of the duties and purposes of the department. He also shall make from time to time such special investigations and reports as may be required of him by the President or either House of Congress, or as he himself may deem necessary and urgent.

Sec. 9. This Act shall take effect March 4, 1925: *Provided, however,* That the provisions of this Act in relation to the transfer of any agency from the jurisdiction and control of one officer to the jurisdiction and control of another, or in relation to the abolishment of any existing agency, or in relation to the transfer of authority, powers, and duties from one officer or agency to another, shall take effect and be in force July 1, 1925, and not before.

Sec. 10. No suit, action, or other proceeding lawfully commenced by or against the head of any department or bureau or other officer of the United States in his official capacity, or in relation to the discharge of his official duties, shall abate by reason of the transfer of authority, powers, and duties from one officer or agency of the Government to another under the provisions of this Act, but the court, on motion or supplemental petition filed at any time within twelve months after this Act shall take effect, showing a necessity for a survival thereof to obtain a settlement of the question involved, may allow the same to be maintained by or against the head of the department or other officer of the United States to whom said authority, powers, and duties are transferred by this Act.

Sec. 11. The head of each executive department is hereby given power and authority to make, subject to the approval of the President, such changes in the organization of the bureaus, offices, and other branches of the public service included in his department as he may deem essential to economical and effective administration; and he is hereby authorized and empowered to reorganize or consolidate, with the approval of the President, any of the bureaus, offices, or other branches of the public service under his jurisdiction, and to set up such divisions, offices, and districts as may be best adapted to accomplish the purposes for which the department was established: *Provided,* That the head of each department shall specially report to Congress at the beginning of each regular session any action taken under the provisions of this section, with the reasons therefor.

THE "HARDING" BILL. *Be it enacted by the Senate and House of Representatives of the United States of America in Congress assembled,* That there is established at the seat of government an executive department to be known as the Department of Education and Welfare for the purpose of protecting and promoting the education, health, and social welfare of the people of the United States. The head of the department shall be the Secretary of Education and Welfare, who shall be appointed by the President, by and with the advice and consent of the Senate. The Secretary of Education and Welfare shall receive an annual salary of $12,000, and his tenure of office shall be the same as that of the heads of the other executive departments.

Sec. 2. That there shall be in the Department of Education and Welfare the following divisions:

(1) A Division of Education, which, under the general supervision of the Secretary, shall have charge of the educational functions and activities of the department and shall, by investigation, publication, and such other methods as may be authorized by Congress, promote the development of schools and other educational and recreational facilities for the instruction of children and illiterate adults, the training of teachers, and the Americanization of those persons in the United States who lack knowledge of our language or institutions;

(2) A Division of Public Health, which, under the general supervision of the Secretary, shall have charge of the health functions and activities of the department and shall by investigation, publication, and such other methods as may be authorized by Congress, protect and promote the public health;

(3) A Division of Social Service, which, under the general supervision of the Secretary, shall have charge of the social welfare functions and activities of the department;

(4) A Division of Veteran Service, which, under the general supervision of the Secretary, shall have charge of the soldiers' and sailors' insurance, compensation, rehabilitation, and pension functions and activities of the department.

Each division of the department shall be in charge of an Assistant Secretary of Education and Welfare, who shall be appointed by the President by and with the advice and consent of the Senate. Each Assistant Secretary shall perform such duties as may be prescribed by the Secretary or required by law and shall receive an annual salary to be determined by Congress: *Provided,* The President in his discretion may more specifically designate said assistant secretaries, one as Assistant Secretary for Education, one as Assistant Secretary for Public Health, one as Assistant Secretary for Social Service, and one as Assistant Secretary for Veteran Service.

There shall also be in the Department of Education and Welfare one chief clerk and a disbursing clerk and such other clerical and other assistants as may from time to time be provided by Congress.

Sec. 3. That section 158 of the Revised Statutes is amended to include the Department of Education and Welfare, and the provisions of Title IV of the Revised Statutes, as amended, are extended and made applicable to the department. The Secretary of Education and Welfare shall cause to be made for the department a seal of such device as the President shall approve, and judicial notice shall be taken of such seal.

Sec. 4. That the office of Commissioner of Education in the Department of the Interior; the office of the Surgeon General in the Treasury Department; the offices of the chief, assistant chief, and private secretary to the chief of the Children's Bureau in the Department of Labor; the office of the Director of the Veterans' Bureau; the Federal Board for Vocational Education; the Board of Managers of the National Home for Disabled Volunteer Soldiers, and the Board of Commissioners of the Soldiers' Home are abolished. All the functions, powers, and duties, which at the time this section takes effect are conferred or imposed by law or lawful Executive order upon any office, board, commission, or other agency abolished by this Act are transferred to, vested in, and imposed upon the Department of Education and Welfare.

Sec. 5. That the bureau called the Office of Education and the Bureau of Pensions in the Department of the Interior, the Public Health Service in the Treasury Department, the Children's Bureau and the bureau known as the Women's Bureau in the Department of Labor, the Freedmen's Hospital, and the National Home for Disabled Volunteer Soldiers are transferred to and shall hereafter be under the jurisdiction and supervision of the Department of Education and Welfare. The functions, powers, and duties which at the time this section takes effect are conferred or imposed by law or lawful Executive order upon the Secretary of the Interior with respect to education or pensions, including the education of Indians, or with respect to the Columbia Institution for the Deaf, the Howard University, or Saint Elizabeth's Hospital are transferred to, vested in, and imposed upon the Secretary of the Department of Education and Welfare.

The functions, powers, and duties which at the time this section takes effect are conferred or imposed by law or lawful

Executive order upon the Secretary of War with respect to the Soldiers' Home are transferred to, vested in, and imposed upon the Secretary of Education and Welfare: *Provided,* That the President in his discretion may by Executive order constitute and may appoint an advisory board of not to exceed seven members to perform, in conjunction with the Secretary of Education and Welfare and in relation to the Soldiers' Home and the National Home for Disabled Volunteer Soldiers, or either of said institutions, such duties as the President or Congress may prescribe.

Sec. 6. That the Smithsonian Institution, an establishment founded at Washington by the Act entitled "An Act to establish the 'Smithsonian Institution' for the increase and diffusion of knowledge among men," approved by the President August 10, 1846, is continued, and, except, as herein otherwise provided, all laws and parts of laws applicable to said establishment at the time of the approval of this Act shall remain in full force and effect until modified, amended, or repealed by Congress. The Board of Regents of the Smithsonian Institution is hereby abolished, and all the functions, powers, and duties which at the time this section takes effect are exercised by or conferred or imposed upon said board are transferred to, vested in, and imposed upon the Department of Education and Welfare. The secretary of the Institution shall be appointed by the President with the advice and consent of the Senate. The secretary's term of office shall be six years or until his successor shall have been appointed and shall qualify.

Sec. 7. That all functions, powers, and duties which at the time this section takes effect are exercised by or conferred or imposed upon any head of an executive department in or over the administration of any office, board, bureau, commission, agency, or institution which by this Act is abolished or transferred to the Department of Education and Welfare, or in or over any business arising from or pertaining to the execution of the powers or the performance of the duties conferred or imposed by law upon such office, board, bureau, commission, or agency, or in relation to the custody, care, or control of any such institution, whether of an apellate or advisory or other character, shall, except as otherwise provided in this

Act, be vested in and exercised and performed by the Secretary of Education and Welfare.

Sec. 8. That section 28 of the Act entitled "An Act to provide compensation for employees of the United States suffering injuries while in the performance of their duties, and for other purposes," approved September 7, 1916, is amended to read as follows:

"Sec. 28. That for the purpose of administration, except as herein otherwise provided, the Commissioner of Pensions be, and is hereby, authorized and directed to perform, or cause to be performed, any and all acts and to make such rules and regulations as may be necessary and proper for the purpose of carrying the provisions of this Act into effect. The commissioner shall, subject to the general supervision and approval of the Secretary of Education and Welfare, administer this Act and perform all the duties and exercise the powers heretofore imposed upon or vested in the United States Employees' Compensation Commission, which said commission is abolished. Whenever in any law, or lawful Executive order, rule, or regulation, there occurs the name of or any reference to the United States Employees' Compensation Commission such name or reference shall be deemed to mean the Commissioner of Pensions."

Sec. 9. That for the purpose of providing for the more efficient and economical administration of the powers, duties, and functions which by this act are transferred to, vested in, and imposed upon the Department of Education and Welfare, the Secretary of Education and Welfare is authorized with the approval of the President to assign all or any part of such functions, powers, or duties to one or more of the divisions created by this Act in the department, and to reorganize, consolidate, or abolish any office, bureau, or other agency which by this Act is transferred to the department, and to set up such new bureaus, agencies, or administrative organizations in his department as may be required to carry out the provisions of this Act. Orders issued by the Secretary in pursuance of the power conferred by this section shall be in writing, shall be filed among the records of the department, and shall be reported by the Secretary to Congress.

Sec. 10. That the President is authorized to transfer to the Department of Education and Welfare, in addition to the functions, powers, and duties transferred to the department by this Act, any educational, health, or social welfare service or activity, performed or conducted by any other office, bureau, board, commission, or agency of the Federal Government, which the President shall find and by proclamation declare are related to or connected with the functions, powers, and duties which by this Act are transferred to and vested in the Department or Secretary of Education and Welfare and would in his judgment be more efficiently and economically administered if vested in, imposed upon, and coördinated with the Department of Education and Welfare. The President's order directing such transfer shall designate the records, equipment, property, personnel, and available balances of appropriations of the office or agency therefore exercising or performing the powers or duties affected by the order, which shall also be transferred to the department. All powers and duties whether of a supervisory, appellate, or other character, conferred or imposed by law or lawful Executive order upon the head of an executive department in relation to the administration of the functions, powers, or duties so transferred, shall be vested in and shall be thereafter exercised and performed by the Secretary of Education and Welfare. The Secretary may assign the functions, powers, and duties so transferred by the President to such division or divisions of the Department of Education and Welfare as he may deem advisable.

Sec. 11. That all records and papers belonging to or on file in and pertaining exclusively to the business of any office, bureau, board, commission, or other agency which is abolished by this Act, or which is transferred to the Department of Education and Welfare, and all furniture, equipment, and other property belonging to the United States in use in, or in the care or custody of, any such office, bureau, board, commission, or other agency, are transferred to the department. The President may, upon the request of the Secretary, direct the transfer to the department of originals or duplicates of other records in any executive department or establishment of the Government, the possession of which he deems necessary to the efficient administration of the department.

Sec. 12.   That all officers and employees under the control and jurisdiction of or employed in or by any office, bureau, board, commission, agency, or institution which under the provisions of this Act is abolished or transferred to the Department of Education and Welfare are transferred to the department at their respective grades and salaries on the date of such transfer: *Provided,* That the transfer of an officer or employee to the Department of Education and Welfare under the provisions of this Act shall not be construed to be a transfer within the meaning of section 7 of the Urgent Deficiency Appropriation Act approved October 6, 1917.   All unexpended balances of appropriations, including continuing, specific, or indefinite appropriations, available at the time this section takes effect for use in the administration of any such office, bureau, board, commission, agency, institution, or building shall be and remain available for expenditure in and by the Department of Education and Welfare for use in the administration of the functions, powers, and duties transferred to the department.

Sec. 13.   That any controversy between the Department of Education and Welfare and any other department or agency of the Federal Government with respect to what functions, powers, duties, records, property, appropriations, or personnel are under the provisions of this Act transferred to the Department of Education and Welfare shall be determined by the President.

Sec. 14.   That the secretary of Education and Welfare shall have charge in the buildings and premises occupied by or appropriated to the Department of Education and Welfare, of the library, furniture, fixtures, records, and other property pertaining to it or hereafter acquired for use in its business. Until other suitable quarters are provided, the Department of Education and Welfare shall occupy the buildings and premises now occupied by the bureaus, offices, and branches of the public service, which by this Act are abolished or transferred to said department.

Sec. 15.   That all Executive orders, rules or regulations issued by any officer or agency of the Federal Government in or in connection with the administration of any function, power or duty which under the provisions of this Act is transferred to the Department of Education and Welfare, and in full force and effect when this section takes effect, are continued in full force and effect and shall be operative until modified, superseded, or repealed by the Secretary of the Department of Education and Welfare. Any permit or other privilege granted prior to the date when this section takes effect by any officer or agency of the Federal Government in or in connection with the administration of any function, power, or duty which under the provisions of this Act is transferred to the Department of Education and Welfare is continued in full force and effect to the same extent as if this Act had not been passed. This Act shall not affect pending cases or proceedings, civil or criminal, brought by or against any office, board, bureau, commission, or any other agency hereby abolished or transferred to the Department of Education and Welfare; but all proceedings, hearings, investigations, and other matters pending in or before any such office, board, bureau, commission, or agency so abolished or transferred shall be continued and brought to final determination before the Secretary or such other officer of the department as may be designated by the Secretary in the same manner as though such office, bureau, board, commission, or agency had been continued as heretofore.

Sec. 16. That whenever in any law, or in any order, rule, or regulation made in pursuance of law, there occurs the name of or any reference to any office, bureau, board, commission, or agency which under the provisions of this Act is abolished or transferred to the Department of Education and Welfare, such name or reference shall be deemed to mean the Department of Education and Welfare as established by this Act.

Sec. 17. That the Secretary of Education and Welfare shall make annually, at the close of each fiscal year, a report in writing to Congress, giving an account of all moneys received and disbursed by him and his department, describing the work done by the department, and making such recommendations as he shall deem necessary for the effective performance of the duties and the accomplishment of the purposes of the department. He shall also make from time to time such special investigations and reports as may be required of him by the President or either House of Congress, or as he may deem necessary.

Sec. 18. That there is hereby appropriated, out of any moneys in the Treasury not otherwise appropriated, the sum of $10,000, or so much thereof as may be necessary to carry out the purposes of this Act during the balance of the fiscal year ending June 30, 1924.

Sec. 19. That sections 4 to 16, both inclusive, of this Act shall take effect July 1, 1924, and the other sections of this Act shall take effect from and after the date of its enactment.

A study of debates upon these measures, special inquiries made from individuals, and examinations of literature gathered here and there, show clearly how little the public, the educators, the social scientists and others know about the meaning, organization and purpose of public welfare. To the new future, therefore, we may look for more study, better understanding, and more effective work.

www.ingramcontent.com/pod-product-compliance
Lightning Source LLC
Chambersburg PA
CBHW021851020426
42334CB00013B/287